SURVEY OF THE SCRIPTURES

PART II

Old Testament Poetry and Prophecy
Job—Malachi

by
ALFRED MARTIN, Th.D.
Dean of Education
Moody Bible Institute

MOODY BIBLE INSTITUTE
CORRESPONDENCE SCHOOL
820 North LaSalle Street
Chicago, Illinois 60610

Copyright ©, 1961, by
THE MOODY BIBLE INSTITUTE
OF CHICAGO

Tenth Printing, 1977

All rights in this course are reserved. No part of this course, whether text, self-check tests or exams, may be reproduced in any manner, including photocopy, without written permission. Permission is not needed for brief quotations embodied in critical articles and reviews.

Printed in the United States of America

Instructions to Students

To see the Scriptures as a whole is not only vital to a proper understanding of the Bible; it can also be a thrilling experience. This course was written by Dr. Alfred Martin, Dean of Education, Moody Bible Institute. It is based in part on a former course by Dr. James M. Gray. Exams, maps and charts were prepared by John Phillips. This textbook is the second in a series of three, designed to take you completely through the Bible.

Part I   Old Testament History
               Genesis—Esther

Part II   Old Testament Poetry and Prophecy
               Job—Malachi

Part III   New Testament
               Matthew—Revelation

HOW PART II IS ORGANIZED

LESSON
13   The Book of Job . . . 169
14   The Book of Psalms . . . 177
15   Proverbs, Ecclesiastes, The Song of Solomon . . . 191
16   Introduction to the Prophetical Books . . . 200
17   Isaiah . . . 215
18   Jeremiah and Lamentations . . . 225
19   Ezekiel . . . 239
20   Daniel . . . 247
21   Hosea, Joel, Amos . . . 261
22   Obadiah, Jonah, Micah . . . 270
23   Nahum, Habakkuk, Zephaniah . . . 285
24   Haggai, Zechariah, Malachi . . . 292

HOW LONG SHOULD IT TAKE?

Study at your own speed. Normally, about two hours are required to complete a lesson—not counting the time spent on Bible reading assignments. You should aim to complete one lesson each week and mail your exams regularly.

HOW TO STUDY

1. Get Ready

Try to find a quiet spot free from distractions and noise, in order to concentrate on your work. Have a pencil with you and underline or mark important words or passages. Look in a dictionary for any words you do not understand.

2. Pray

Since the Bible is God's Book, you need the help of the Holy Spirit if you are to understand it. Psalm 119:18, if prayed from the heart, would be an appropriate prayer to use: "Open thou mine eyes, that I may behold wondrous things out of thy law."

3. Read, Study, Meditate and Apply

Read the lesson in the textbook thoroughly, looking up Scripture references in their context in order to understand them. Read, reread, study and think about what you have read until you grasp the themes and outlines presented. Always apply practical truths to yourself. The more light you have on God's Word, the more responsible you are to live up to it.

4. Reading Assignments

A complete reading of the Bible is essential to proper Bible survey. Read each book of the Bible in the light of the outlines in your textbook. At the end of each exam (not self-check test) you will find a READING CHART which lists the Scripture readings covering the books of the Bible you are studying. As you read the Bible book, or books, covered by each lesson, check the chapters (×) on the READING CHART. This will enable your instructor to give you a correct grade for each exam, as ten points are allowed for each reading assignment. You cannot obtain a grade of 100 per cent on an exam in this course if you do not complete the reading assignments.

EXAMS AND SELF-CHECK TESTS

Odd-numbered lessons are followed by self-check tests, and even-numbered lessons are followed by exams which cover the two preceding lessons.

1. Self-Check Tests

These are sometimes in two parts. *The first part* deals with the factual content of the lesson you have just studied, and is intended to help you evaluate your progress before proceeding to the next lesson. You may use your tests as an aid to study; but when you actually fill in the answers, you should do so without referring to your textbook. *The second part* is captioned DIG DEEPER IN YOUR BIBLE and contains questions you will not normally be able to answer from the textbook itself. They are intended for more serious study. They are more difficult and will be more of a challenge to you. They will help you discover important Bible truths and see the amazing unity of the content of the Word of God. A complete answer key to all self-check tests is given on pages 309, 310. When you have answered all the questions, check your answers and evaluate your progress. Be sure to restudy the textbook to correct your mistakes before going on to the next lesson. Do not send answers to self-check tests to the Correspondence School.

2. Exams

After every second lesson, you will find a complete exam covering the two preceding lessons and marked accordingly. Turn to this exam, after you have read the lessons two or three times, and see how well you know the answers. (It is recommended that you take an exam after you have studied both of the lessons covered by it. If at times you prefer taking the exam in two sections, that is, one lesson at a time, you may do so.) Glance through the lesson, or lessons, until you are sure you can answer all the questions on the exam, or section of the exam. Since some questions are based on the maps and charts in your textbook, be sure you have mastered those which apply before you begin the exam. When you are sure you can answer all the questions, you are ready to take the exam.

Many of the exams have a section called USE YOUR BIBLE. The answers to these questions are not usually to be found in the textbook but will have to be sought in the Bible itself. These questions are often more difficult than the others, and are intended to challenge you and teach you important truths you might otherwise miss.

In taking the exam, follow this procedure:

a. **Write the Exam.** Complete it according to instructions and without referring to your textbook or notes. Use pen and dark ink. Use your Bible only if instructions tell you to do so.

b **Detach the Exam.** When you have completed both sections of the exam (that is, when you have answered all the questions relating to two lessons), detach the exam from your textbook. If you are careful, you will find that the pages may be taken out without spoiling your textbook.

c. **Mail Your Exam to the Correspondence School.**

d. Keep Your Exams for Future Use. Some of your exams contain valuable charts which you will have helped to complete. To keep your exams for future reference, put them in a three-ring notebook.

CLASS ENROLLMENTS

If you are enrolled in a class, submit your exam papers to the leader or secretary of the class, who will send them for the group to the Correspondence School.

Class leaders are to print or type the names of all students enrolled in the course on the Class Record Sheet. Before returning corrected exams to the students, the class leader must record the grades on the Class Record Sheet. Each student should also keep a record of his own grades on the Grade Record Card found in the front of each textbook. When the last exam is taken, the completed Class Record Sheet must be returned to the Correspondence School. The grades of *all* completed exams must be recorded, with the exception of the final ones being returned with the Class Record Sheet. Without this information it will not be possible to issue certificates. For example, if you are sending in Exam 6 for correction, the Class Record Sheet must show the grades of Exams 1-5 for all students who have completed them. If a student finishes the course after the Class Record Sheet has been sent in, he should send us his completed Grade Record Card. This card must bear an accurate record of the student's *grades, class number,* and *signature.*

GENERAL INSTRUCTIONS

1. Each exam has 45 parts; two points are allowed for each part. An extra 10 points can be earned by completing the Scripture reading assignments.

    Upon completing Part II of this course with a passing average of 70 percent or more, you will be awarded a certificate.

2. The Authorized (or King James) Version is used in this course, except for an occasional quotation from the American Standard Version, published in 1901. These quotations are indicated by the abbreviation, A.S.V. These are the only versions you are permitted to use in answering the exam questions.

3. The Correspondence School staff meets weekly for united prayer on behalf of students sending special prayer requests. Feel free to send these at any time. When sending in prayer requests, please write them on a separate piece of paper.

4. You will be allowed one year to complete the course from the time of enrollment. Your name will then be removed from the roll and you will not be able to earn a certificate for the course without complete re-enrollment.

RECORD YOUR GRADES

At the front of this book you will find a Grade Record Card. Each time you receive a corrected exam from the Correspondence School, make a careful note of the grade in the appropriate place on the card. When sending in your last exam, return this Grade Record Card to us so that we can issue you a certificate. Make sure that all grades are recorded on this card with the exception of the final exam(s) you are enclosing. This is most important.

Lesson 13

The Book of Job

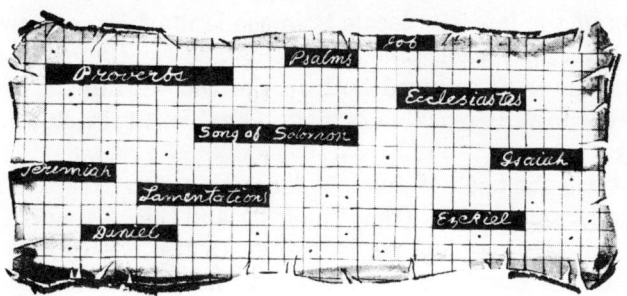

INTRODUCTION TO THE POETICAL BOOKS

The five books—Job, Psalms, Proverbs, Ecclesiastes, and Song of Solomon—are generally called the poetical books because in their form they are poetry rather than prose. With these may be included the book of Lamentations, which is also poetical in form, although found in a different section of the Old Testament. The term *poetical* does not mean fanciful or unreal, but refers merely to the style. Poetry has always been recognized as the language of the heart, and these are books of experience in which the longings and aspirations of the people of God are evident.

The chief characteristic of Hebrew poetry is neither rhyme nor rhythm, but a kind of "sense rhythm" or repetition of ideas, usually known as *parallelism*. Because of this quality, Hebrew poetry can be translated into all the different languages without losing its poetic form. While there are many kinds of parallelism, the three most common kinds are *synonymous*, in which a thought is stated and then repeated in similar language; *antithetic*, in which a thought is stated and is followed by its contrast; and *synthetic*, in which a number of related thoughts are built into a structural form.

The American Standard Version is helpful in that it prints the poetical books in poetic form.

THE BOOK OF JOB

The book of Job is generally thought to be one of the oldest portions of the Word of God. The human writer is unknown. The life which is described seems to belong to the patriarchal period, that is, in the time between Abraham and the giving of the law. Its locale is in the land of Uz, somewhere to the east of Israel. The book is named for the chief character, who is recognized both in the Old Testament and in the New as a historical personage (Ezekiel 14:14, 20; James 5:11).

In form the book of Job is a dramatic poem except for the opening two chapters (the prologue) and the closing chapter (the epilogue) which are in prose. In the poetical portion the action is carried on by means of dialogue.

1. Purpose of the Book

The great question posed by this book is, Why do the righteous suffer? The problem of suffering is a universal one. God does not answer the question abstractly or theoretically, but through the concrete experience of a righteous man.

Through the prologue we are allowed to know the answer, at least dimly, from the very beginning. Yet many Bible students persist in making the same mistakes that Job's three "friends" made. They overlook the fact that God called Job a perfect and upright man (1:1; 1:8; 2:3), asserting that there was no one like him in all the world and that the suffering which he endured was not caused by anything within himself. One cannot understand or appreciate the book of Job without accepting God's estimate of the man.

2. Structure of the Book

Job is in five parts, the first and last of which are in prose, as we have seen.

    I. PROLOGUE (WHAT TOOK PLACE IN HEAVEN) (chapters 1 and 2)

    II. THE CONTROVERSY OF JOB WITH HIS THREE FRIENDS (chapters 3—31)

III. THE WORDS OF ELIHU (chapters 32—37)
IV. THE ANSWER OF THE LORD (chapters 38—41)
V. EPILOGUE ("THE END OF THE LORD," James 5:11) (chapter 42)

3. Prologue (What Took Place in Heaven) (chapters 1 and 2)

Comment has already been made concerning God's estimate of Job. This book shows the reality of Satan and pictures him in a role which Scripture elsewhere describes as "the accuser of . . . [the] brethren" (Revelation 12:10). Satan's theory is that Job served God only because God had blessed him and had given him many gifts. There is comfort for the child of God in the knowledge that Satan cannot get at him without God's express permission. For once, strangely enough, the devil, the "father of lies," tells the truth when he says to God concerning Job, "Hast not thou made an hedge about him, and about his house, and about all that he hath on every side?" (1:10).

Two tests are permitted by God. In the first, Job loses his possessions and his children. In the second, Job himself is afflicted with a painful and loathsome disease. In each case God says that Job did not sin with his lips (1:22; 2:10). This is the background. The prologue ends with the arrival of Job's three friends, Eliphaz, Bildad, and Zophar, who come "to mourn with him and to comfort him" (2:11).

4. The Controversy of Job with His Three Friends (chapters 3—31)

In this lengthy section there are three cycles of discussion. Job speaks; then each of the friends speaks in turn, being answered in each case by Job.

a. The First Cycle (chapters 3—14)
b. The Second Cycle (chapters 15—21)
c. The Third Cycle (chapters 22—31)

While the three friends have emphases differing from one another, their basic premise is the same, that Job is suffering because he is a great sinner. As the discussion progresses, the friends become more severe in their condemnation of Job. Bildad speaks more sternly than Eliphaz, and Zophar yet more sternly. In the second round of the discussion the intensity of their condemnation increases. This time Zophar speaks only briefly, while in the third round, the harshest of all, Bildad cuts his words short and Zophar does not even speak, apparently considering that Job is beyond help.

Much that the friends say is true, as Job gladly acknowledges, concerning the great principle of sin and retribution. It is true that sin brings punishment, which, of course, entails suffering. The mistake of the friends is in thinking that all suffering is the result of personal sin. The only explanation to their limited understanding is that sin brings suffering; therefore a man who is suffering as much as Job is has to be a great sinner.

Although Job is perplexed and complains bitterly that he cannot understand the *why* of his suffering, he does not claim to be sinless. He protests, however, that his friends do not have the true explanation. Bildad, in his first speech, plainly states that he considers Job a hypocrite (compare 8:13). Zophar goes even further and calls Job a liar (11:3). In his answer to the friends in this first cycle, Job uses sarcasm (12:2) and points out that the things which they have said about sin and suffering are common knowledge, but are not the answer to his problem.

After Eliphaz has spoken the second time, Job calls his friends "miserable comforters" (16:2). Although he is troubled and perplexed and is constantly asking why, nevertheless Job's faith is sublime and real, reaching its height in the wonderful words, "For I know that my redeemer liveth" (19:25).

To the statement that suffering always is the result of sin, Job poses the counter problem of the admittedly wicked man who seemingly enjoys prosperity throughout his life. The friends can only maintain their original theory that suffering is penal. Eliphaz accuses Job of infinite iniquities (22:5).

5. The Words of Elihu (chapters 32—37)

Elihu, a young man who had stood by listening to the controversy of Job and his three friends, now can restrain himself no longer. He does not approve either of what the friends have said or of what Job has said. Elihu is much nearer to the solution of the problem than were the three friends. His premise throughout his speech is that suffering is remedial. Through it God is disciplining and teaching. He believes that Job has accused God unjustly.

Scripture makes it plain that some suffering is penal and that some suffering is remedial. Much of what Job's three friends have said is true; much that Elihu said is true; but even Elihu does not have the final answer to the problem of the book. God has set down by inspiration exactly what each of these persons has said. But this does not mean that everything which they said is God's thought upon the matter. In fact, in the epilogue God clearly states that the friends have not spoken the thing which is right. Hence we must be very careful, in quoting from the book of Job, that we do not take a quotation from its context and misapply it. Every word set down in the book is inspired of God. This is true even of the words of Satan; yet we would not quote these words of Satan by themselves as though they were what God had to say.

6. The Answer of the LORD (chapters 38—41)

The text plainly says that the LORD answered Job (38:1). The strangest and most obvious thing about this answer is that it consists of a series of questions. Not once does God actually explain to Job the reason for his suffering. Instead He asks Job questions concerning his knowledge of the natural world, with the clear implication that, since Job cannot even answer these questions, he is clearly out of his depth in seeking to answer questions about the spiritual realm. This answer of the LORD as it continues (40:1) causes Job to realize his own littleness and worthlessness (40:4), and finally brings him in the closing chapter to abhorrence of himself and repentance (42:6). Job finally discovers that he does not need to know *why* if he knows God. A true vision of God gave to him a true vision of himself as well.

Some will maintain that this proves the point of the three friends that Job really was a sinner, but we must not overlook the words spoken by God Himself in the prologue. The truth is presented that those who know God best are most conscious of their own worthlessness, that the greatest saints are those who know best their own innate sinfulness. So it was with Isaiah when he saw the LORD (Isaiah 6), with Daniel by the River Hiddekel (Daniel 10), with John on the Isle of Patmos (Revelation 1:9). After he was a Christian for many years, Paul testified, "For I know that in me (that is, in my flesh,) dwelleth no good thing" (Romans 7:18).

7. Epilogue ("The End of the Lord") (chapter 42)

God is fully vindicated and glorified against the slander of Satan. Some suffering is for punishment; some is for teaching; but there is a higher purpose in some suffering. It is for the glory of God, which is the most important consideration in the universe. James tells us, "Ye have heard of the patience [endurance] of Job, and have seen the end of the Lord; that the Lord is very pitiful, and of tender mercy" (James 5:11). In the closing section of the book God, who always delights to give to His own, gives to Job twice as much as he had before (42:10). God is glorified in a human life, and the implication is that Job's experience is not unique. Satan has similarly accused others and God has been vindicated in the lives of many of His children.

Self Check Test 7

What do you know about Bible poetry?
(See page 165 for instructions.)

In the right-hand column circle the following statements "true" or "false":

1. The controversy between Job and his friends is covered in three cycles of discussion. (p. 171) T F

2. The harshest of Job's critics was Elihu. (p. 172) T F

3. Job denied everything his friends said. (p. 172) T F

4. Job's friends were very comforting to him. (p. 172) T F

5. There are only five books in the Bible which are poetical in form. (p. 169) T F

The three most common forms of parallelism in Bible poetry have been termed (a) synonymous, (b) antithetic, (c) synthetic.

Circle the letter of the form of parallelism defined in each of the following:

6. Poetry in which a number of related thoughts are built into a structural form   a   b   c

7. Poetry in which a thought is stated and then repeated in similar language   a   b   c

8. Poetry in which a thought is stated and is followed by a contrast (p. 169)   a   b   c

Circle the letter of the correct statement.

9. The person who came closest to the solution of Job's problem was

   a. Elihu.

   b. Bildad.

   c. Eliphaz.

   d. Zophar (p. 173).

10. In quoting from the book of Job, we

    a. must always note whose words we are quoting.

    b. may freely quote any part of it as truth since it is in the Bible.

    c. should refuse to regard it as inspired since it contains some statements which are untrue.

    d. are always on safe ground (p. 173).

11. Hebrew poetry is characterized by

    a. rhyme and rhythm.

    b. the repetition of ideas.

    c. phonetic equations.

    d. duplications of sound (p. 169).

12. Job was

    a. a righteous man.

    b. a hypocrite.

    c. a heathen.

    d. suffering because he was a great sinner (p. 170).

Turn to page 309 to find the correct answers.
Do not send the answers to the Correspondence School.

Lesson 14

The Book of Psalms

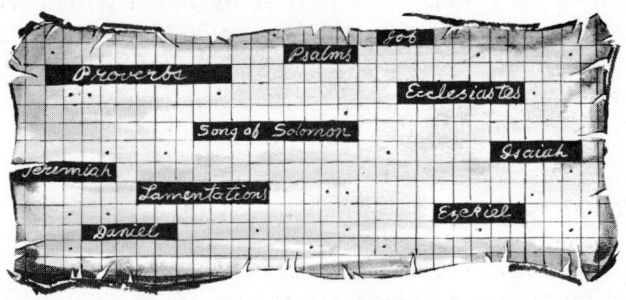

If Christians had to give up all the books of the Old Testament except one, and were allowed to choose the one which they could keep, undoubtedly more people would choose Psalms than any other book. This is seen also in the fact that many of our editions of the New Testament include the book of Psalms as well. This book is quoted more often in the New Testament than any other Old Testament book.

THE TITLE OF THE BOOK

The original Hebrew title of the book of Psalms is a word which means "praises." This is an appropriate description of the content of the book. It is a collection of songs of praise to God. The title *Psalms*, given to the book in the Greek translation, the Septuagint Version, means "songs." In the Greek language the word *psalm* means a song set to instrumental accompaniment. Hence, this title which we use describes the form of the book rather than its content. It is a collection of one hundred and fifty different songs, largely songs of praises.

THE HUMAN WRITERS OF THE PSALMS

The principal human writer of the Psalms is David, described in Scripture as "the sweet psalmist of Israel" (II Samuel 23:1). Many of the Psalms have titles indicating authorship, and in these titles, seventy-three Psalms are ascribed to David. In addition, two others, Psalms 2 and 95, are attributed to David as they are quoted in the New Testament (Acts 4:25; Hebrews 4:7). Hence, we can say that at least half of the Psalms were written by David. Other writers were Asaph, twelve Psalms (Psalm 50 and Psalms 73—83); Solomon, two Psalms (72 and 127, A.S.V.); Moses, one (Psalm 90); Heman, one (Psalm 88); and Ethan, one (Psalm 89). Many of the Psalms are anonymous.

THE PSALTER—AN INSPIRED HYMNBOOK

The book of Psalms or the Psalter, as it is often called, is an inspired hymnbook setting forth the thoughts, feelings and aspirations of the people of God in every conceivable kind of circumstance. Every emotion is described, from the most sublime joy to the deepest gloom. This is indeed a book of experience. The Holy Spirit, working in and through the human writers without doing violence to their personalities, enables them to set down exactly what He wishes them to write—but not something external to themselves; rather, their innermost thoughts, thus reaching the hearts of men.

THE THEMES OF THE PSALMS

The themes of the Psalms are exceedingly varied. Hence, it is difficult in a few words to survey their content. Many of the Psalms are prophetic, and the most prominent theme in the book is that of the coming Saviour, the Messiah, the Lord Jesus Christ. Psalms which speak prophetically of Christ are called *Messianic Psalms*. There are at least thirteen of these quoted specifically in the New Testament as referring to Christ (Psalms 2, 8, 16, 22, 31, 40, 41, 45, 68, 69, 102, 110, 118). There are undoubtedly many others which are Messianic, although not specifically quoted as such in the New Testament. These would include the familiar twenty-third Psalm, which can be linked with the statement of the Lord Jesus Christ in John 10:11 concerning Himself as the Good Shepherd. Psalm 22, often referred to as the Psalm of the cross, reveals to us the thoughts of the Lord Jesus Christ as He bore our sins in His own body on the tree, crying out when God made Him to be sin for us (II Corinthians 5:21), "My God, my God, why hast thou forsaken me?" (compare Matthew 27:46).

Some of the Psalms are *Nature Psalms,* but these differ from many of the poems of nature in world literature in that in the Scripture nature is never celebrated for its own sake, but only as it points to its Creator, God Himself. Some of the familiar Nature Psalms are 8 (which is also Messianic), 19, 29, 33 and 104.

There are a number of *Historical Psalms,* in which the history of God's people is recounted as a reminder of God's faithfulness and as a lesson to present and future generations to trust and obey God. The great period of Israel's history most often celebrated in the Psalms is the period of the Exodus from Egypt and the wilderness wanderings. Some of the Historical Psalms are 78, 105 and 106.

In their prophetic aspects, many Psalms look forward to the future reign of Christ upon the earth. While these could in a sense be called Messianic Psalms, they are often classified as a separate type, *Millennial Psalms,* such as 46, 72 and 89, among many others.

Another theme running through the Psalms is that of confession and repentance. The leading *Penitential Psalms* are 6, 32 and 51.

The Word of God is another subject which engrossed the psalmists. The longest and best-known Psalm of the Word is, of course, Psalm 119, which in form is an alphabetical Psalm. Its one hundred and seventy-six verses are divided into twenty-two sections of eight verses each. Each section of the Psalm corresponds to a letter of the Hebrew alphabet, and in the Hebrew Bible all the verses in each section begin with the letter of that section. This cannot be shown in translation. Almost every verse describes some feature of the Word of God. Another Psalm on the Word is 19, which is also a Nature Psalm, showing the testimony to God, both in nature and in the Bible. Psalm 1, a fitting introduction to the whole Psalter, also describes the attitude of the godly man toward the Word.

A group of fifteen Psalms, called the *Songs of Degrees* (or *Ascents,* A.S.V.), evidently were used at the time of the pilgrimages to Jerusalem for the annual feasts. All of the Psalms were originally set to music and undoubtedly most of them were sung at various times in the public worship of the people of Israel.

These are only some of the many themes in the book. Throughout, there are the notes of praise and thanksgiving, adoration of God for what He is in Himself and gratitude to Him for what He has done for men. While the setting of the Psalms is Israelitish, and many of the promises are earthly promises to the nation of Israel, there are nevertheless spiritual promises which belong to all the people of God in all dispensations. Many of the notes of praise, and particularly those statements concerning the universal kingdom of God, will be most appropriately sung in the time of the millennial kingdom, when Israel will be restored to the place which God wanted for His chosen people.

THE FIVE BOOKS OF THE PSALMS

In the Hebrew Bible the book of Psalms is actually subdivided into five books. This division is seen in the American Standard Version and in special editions, such as the Scofield Reference Bible. The five books of the Psalms are as follows:

    Book I   Psalms 1—41
    Book II   Psalms 42—72
    Book III   Psalms 73—89
    Book IV   Psalms 90—106
    Book V   Psalms 107—150

Each of these books ends with a special doxology or ascription of praise to God. While there is difference of opinion among scholars concerning the reason for this fivefold division, it is rather generally believed that those men who placed the Psalms in their present order in ancient times thought of these five books as corresponding to the five books of the law. One might think of the following general themes for these five books:

Book I	Creation and Man
Book II	Redemption
Book III	The Sanctuary
Book IV	The Earthly Pilgrimage
Book V	The Word of God

One can see that these are appropriate parallels to Genesis, Exodus, Leviticus, Numbers, and Deuteronomy, respectively.

THE PSALMS—TO BE EXPERIENCED

As has been intimated before, the book of Psalms does not lend itself easily to survey treatment. The Psalms must be experienced. One must read and reread and, like the blessed man described in the opening Psalm, one must meditate continually upon the Word of God. This Psalm of the two ways, as it is sometimes called, with its contrasts between the blessed man and the ungodly, is echoed and re-echoed throughout the Psalter as we see the experiences of those who trust in God and the contrasting experiences of the wicked.

"THE HALLELUJAH PSALMS"

The doxology at the close of Book V is not a single verse, or even a few verses, but a group of five Psalms (146—150) called collectively "The Hallelujah Psalms" because each begins and ends with that Hebrew word. *Hallelujah,* an imperative form, means "Praise ye Jehovah." Here is an appropriate climax to this book of praises, culminating in that appeal for universal praise, "Let every thing that hath breath praise the LORD. Hallelujah."

Reading Chart Example (see page 190)

Check (×) the chapters you have read.

If, for example, you read all of Job but only 91 of the psalms your chart would look like this:

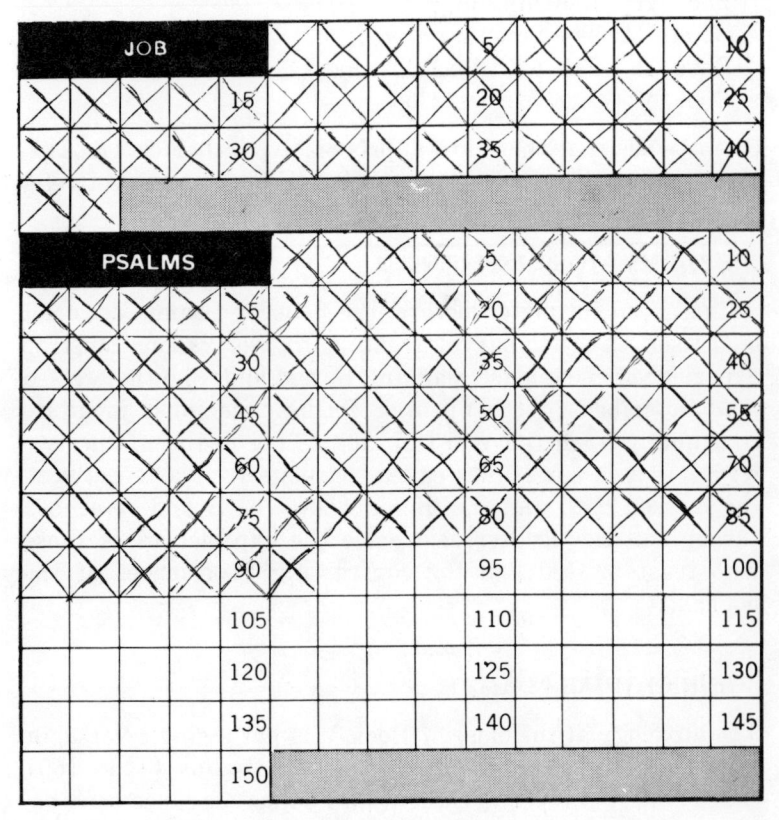

Survey of the Scriptures   *Exam 7*
A Moody Correspondence Course   *Lessons 13, 14*

Name_____ Exam Grade_____
        (Print plainly)

Address_____ Date_____

City_____ State____ Zip Code_____ Class Number_____

Instructor_____

LESSON 13   THE POETICAL BOOKS

In the blank space at the right-hand margin write "True" or "False" after each of the following statements:

EXAMPLE:

The author of the course is Dr. Alfred Martin.   *True*

1. The book of Job is thought to be one of the oldest in the Bible. _____

2. The book of Job is named after its writer. _____

3. All of Job is written in poetic style. _____

4. The great theme of Job is, Why do the righteous suffer? _____

5. Satan declared that Job served God only for what he could get out of Him. _____

183

6. *Complete the following outline of Job:*

		Chapters
I.	Prologue (What Took Place in Heaven)	1 and 2
II.	_____	3—31
III.	_____	32—37
IV.	_____	38—41
V.	_____	42

7. a. According to the textbook what was God's purpose in asking Job questions about the natural world?

   _____

   _____

   _____

   _____

   b. Give two Scripture references outside of the book of Job which show that he was an actual historical figure.

   _____

   _____

Use Your Bible

You may use your Bible to complete the next question.

8. The three most common forms of parallelism used in Bible poetry have been termed <u>synonymous</u>, <u>antithetic</u>, and <u>synthetic</u>. Turn to the following Scripture passages and in the blank space list the form used in each passage.

   a. Proverbs 27:6 _____

   b. Psalm 92:12-15 _____

   c. Proverbs 17:22 _____

   d. Psalm 46:1 _____

   e. Psalm 135:15-18 _____

LESSON 14   THE BOOK OF PSALMS

In the blank space at the right-hand margin write "True" or "False" after each of the following statements:

9. The book of Psalms is quoted in the New Testament more than any other Old Testament book. _____

10. The title given to the book of Psalms describes its content rather than its form. _____

11. The book of Psalms is really a book of hymns. _____

12. The doxology with which the book of Psalms closes is made up of a group of five psalms. _____

13. "Hallelujah" simply means "Amen." _____

14. List three additional writers for the book of Psalms besides David.

   a. _____

   b. _____

   c. _____

In the blank space write the letter of the correct or most nearly correct answer.

EXAMPLE:

The author of this course is

a. Dr. Alfred Martin.
b. John Smith.
c. Peter Brown.
d. Dr. James Jones.   *a*
                                    _____

15. David, who wrote about half of the Psalms, is described in the Bible as

    a. "the sweet psalmist of Israel."
    b. making melody in his heart.
    c. making a joyful noise unto the Lord.
    d. "the father of all such as handle the harp."   _____

16. Which one of the following groups contains three Millennial Psalms?

    a. 28, 52, 89
    b. 48, 52, 60
    c. 34, 45, 91
    d. 46, 72, 89   _____

17. The book of Psalms reflects mainly
    a. imaginative poetry.
    b. emotional experience.
    c. cold facts.
    d. vague longings. _____

Thought and Research

You may use your Bible and textbook for the rest of this exam.

18. Given below are some of the things we could know about the Lord Jesus Christ, if we had only the Messianic Psalms. In the blank space opposite each item write the supporting Scripture reference from one of the thirteen Messianic Psalms listed in the textbook.

    a. *His deity*

    He is absolutely God (compare Hebrews 1:8). _____

    He is God the Son. _____

    b. *His humanity*

    He stooped to take on humanity (compare Hebrews 2:9). _____

    He came voluntarily, delighting in God's will and Word. _____

    c. *His character*

    He showed passion for righteousness and hatred of sin. _____

    He had zeal for the house of God. _____

d. *His rejection by the people*

    He was plotted against and slandered by His foes. _____

    He was the rejected "Stone" destined to be the chief corner stone in God's purposes. _____

e. *His sufferings and death*

    His hands and feet were pierced. _____

    He was despised by the people. _____

    He was given vinegar and gall to drink in His agony. _____

    He was abandoned by God. _____

    His death was substitutionary for He bore our reproaches. _____

f. *His resurrection and ascension*

    His dead body was not allowed to corrupt. _____

    He ascended to heaven. _____

g. *His coming again in power*

    There will be a universal revolt against God. _____

    He will subdue the heathen with a rod of iron. _____

Many of the Psalms can best be understood when studied in the light of the circumstances which gave them birth.

Study carefully the incidents in the life of David, recorded in the Scripture references in questions 19, 20 and 21. Which psalm listed below was written after David's experience on each occasion? Write the letter of the psalm in the proper blank space.

    a. Psalm 52

    b. Psalm 59

    c. Psalm 18

    d. Psalm 54

    e. Psalm 51

19. I Samuel 21:1-10; 22:7-23 _____

20. II Samuel 22:1-51 _____

21. II Samuel 11:1—12:16 _____

Reading Chart

Check (×) the chapters you have read.

	JOB					5				10
			15			20				25
			30			35				40
	PSALMS					5				10
			15			20				25
			30			35				40
			45			50				55
			60			65				70
			75			80				85
			90			95				100
			105			110				115
			120			125				130
			135			140				145
			150							

_____MAIL TO ADDRESS ON BACK COVER.

Lesson 15

Proverbs—Ecclesiastes—The Song of Solomon

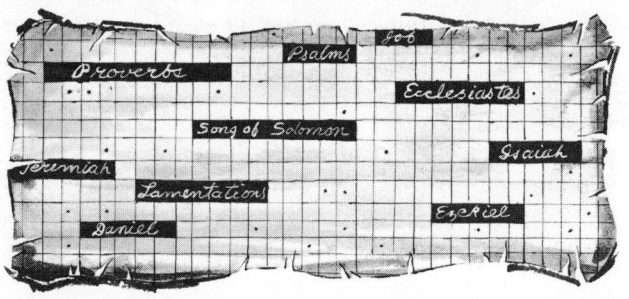

The three books to be studied in this lesson have in common the fact that they are poetical books and that they were written by the same writer, Solomon.

PROVERBS

A proverb is a statement which contains much truth in a few words, expressed in such a way as to gain attention and to stay in the memory. The principal writer of the book is Solomon (1:1; 10:1; 25:1). The Scripture speaks elsewhere of the wisdom that God gave to Solomon and of the fact that he wrote many proverbs (I Kings 4:29-34). Some of these proverbs at least were not collected in their present arrangement until the time of King Hezekiah (25:1). The last two chapters were written by Agur (chapter 30) and Lemuel (chapter 31). Nothing is known concerning either of these men.

1. The Themes of Proverbs

The themes of Proverbs are very numerous. The purpose of the book is to impart wisdom (1:2-4). Wisdom in the Scripture is not mere knowledge, not simply an intellectual quality, but rather a moral and spiritual use of knowledge in subjection to the will of God. "The fear of the LORD is the beginning of wisdom" (9:10). In addition to the prevailing theme in praise of wisdom as opposed to folly, we find many proverbs which teach obedience to parents, the value of friendship, the importance of good company, honesty and industry; and many which warn against laziness, talebearing, lying, evil companions, drunkenness and pride. These are only a few of the dozens of subjects treated in the book. Proverbs is not the kind of book that can be surveyed in the way in which a historical book can, since it is purposely composed of many disconnected topics. It is pre-eminently the young man's book (1:4), giving heavenly instruction as applied to practical, earthly matters.

2. An Outline of Proverbs

I. WISDOM AND FOLLY CONTRASTED (chapters 1—9)

II. MISCELLANEOUS PROVERBS OF SOLOMON ON VARIED THEMES (chapters 10—24)

III. PROVERBS OF SOLOMON COPIED BY "THE MEN OF HEZEKIAH" (chapters 25—29)

IV. "THE WORDS OF AGUR" (chapter 30)

V. "THE WORDS OF KING LEMUEL" (chapter 31)

The only part of the book which can be characterized by one predominant theme is the first division (chapters 1—9). Often in this contrast of wisdom with folly, wisdom is personified as a noble lady who calls upon the young man to give heed to her instruction, as contrasted with the foolish woman who would lead him astray. The Christian reader of the book, comparing Scripture with Scripture, will note that in the New Testament wisdom is not only personified in a figurative way, but is actually found in a Person, the Lord Jesus Christ, "who of God is made unto us wisdom" (I Corinthians 1:30).

In the second division of the book (chapters 10—24),

containing miscellaneous proverbs of Solomon on varied themes, those in chapters 10—15 are mostly antithetic parallelisms, while in chapters 16—24 the synonymous form of parallelism predominates. (Refer back to Lesson 13 for the main kinds of parallelism.)

Hezekiah, whose men copied out proverbs of Solomon (chapters 25—29), was a godly king who lived two centuries after Solomon's time. The men mentioned here (Proverbs 25:1) may possibly be the prophets Isaiah and Micah, who were contemporaries of Hezekiah.

The last twenty-two verses of Proverbs 31, in praise of the virtuous woman, are alphabetical, in that each verse begins with a consecutive letter of the Hebrew alphabet, from the first to the last.

Frequent rereading of the Proverbs is far more profitable than reading comments about them. Here are principles of divine wisdom which can be applied to everyday living. We are assured in God's Word that all Scripture is profitable (II Timothy 3:16). The one who reads and observes the instructions of this book will experience the profitableness in new and increasingly wonderful ways.

ECCLESIASTES

1. The Title of the Book

Although the title of this book, as we have it in our English Bible, is a Greek word, it is a satisfactory translation of the original Hebrew title and means, as the subheading indicates, "The Preacher," one who gathers together a congregation to give instruction and counsel.

2. The Writer

Although the name of Solomon is not specifically mentioned in the book, it seems obvious that he is the writer. He was the son of David. He was king in Jerusalem. He had the background implied throughout the book and the experience necessary to write it.

3. A Perplexing but Inspired Book

This is a perplexing book to many people because, on the surface at least, many of its conclusions seem to be at variance with other parts of Scripture. Yet we know that this is a part of the Word of God, for all of the books which we call the Old Testament had been collected together before the time of the Lord Jesus Christ and were in their entirety endorsed by Him (compare Luke 24:44).

4. The Key Phrase

In order to be understood properly, this book needs a key, and God has given the key—not once, but many times. It is in the phrase, "under the sun," found twenty-nine times in the book. The theme is expressed in 1:2, 3. The word *vanity* means "futility" or "emptiness," and the point that is made throughout the book is that life lived under the sun, that is, on the purely natural plane, is futile. Nothing in this world can fully satisfy the longings of the human heart. "What profit hath a man of all his labor which he taketh under the sun?" (1:3).

5. The Inadequacy of Philosophy to Solve Life's Problems

In this book God permitted Solomon to be a philosopher in order that He might show the inadequacy of philosophy to solve the problems of life. The conclusions concerning the emptiness of life are true when viewed by human observation "under the sun," but far from the truth as it is in Christ Jesus.

In philosophy the two main methods of acquiring knowledge are empiricism and rationalism. Empiricism in the strict sense of the term is the belief that the only valid knowledge comes through sensory experience. Rationalism, on the other hand, is the view that the only valid knowledge comes through the reason. Solomon, in the experiences recorded in the book, makes full use of both of these philosophical methods. Repeatedly he says, "I saw." This is empiricism, depending upon the senses for knowledge. Likewise he says repeatedly, "I said in mine heart," and other similar expressions. This is rationalism, seeking to discover truth through the human reason. That both of these methods are unable to fathom ultimate truths, is attested by the conclusions of the book itself and by many other portions of Scripture. "But as it is written, Eye hath not seen, nor ear heard, neither have entered into the heart of man, the things which God hath prepared for them that love him" (I Corinthians 2:9). By this statement God rules out both empiricism and rationalism as means for attaining the truth of God. This the preacher discovered through his long, discouraging and frustrating experiments. He sought satisfaction in nature, in philosophy, in pleasure, in material possessions, in riches, in accomplishments, in philanthropy, in ethics and so on. Over everything he had to write "emptiness." "Vanity of vanities, saith the preacher; all is vanity" (12:8). Even this experience, however, was enough to show him the necessity of reverence toward God and obedience to Him. The beautiful closing chapter calls upon the young to remember their Creator while they are young, before advancing age closes their opportunities. The preacher recognizes the duty of obeying God in view of a coming judgment (12:13, 14).

6. The Truth of God Given by Supernatural Revelation

Were the book of Ecclesiastes the only portion of God's Word which we had, we should be perplexed and even in despair, knowing the futility of life apart from God and realizing that God will bring every work into judgment. We could not, from this book alone, find the full way of escape. Against this dark background, the grace of God manifested in other parts of His Word shines out more brightly. "But God hath revealed them unto us by his Spirit" (I Corinthians 2:10). That which cannot be known either by senses or by reason has been supernaturally revealed to us by God in His Word.

THE SONG OF SOLOMON

The inspired title of this book is "The Song of Songs" (1:1). Solomon is declared to be the writer. In I Kings 4:32 we are told that Solomon wrote one thousand and five songs. The idiomatic expression, "the song of songs," means that this is the best and greatest of all of Solomon's songs.

Here again we find much that is perplexing. God is not mentioned in the book, except by a very indirect reference to His name in 8:6, which is not even apparent in the Authorized Version (compare A.S.V.). To some people the language of the song seems indelicate or even indecent; yet this cannot be, for the book is indeed a part of the Word of God. In fact, the ancient Hebrews considered it particularly sacred. Of the five books called *the rolls*, which have been read from ancient times on sacred days, The Song of Songs is read in the synagogues annually at the Passover, the first great feast of the Hebrew religious year.

1. Three Interpretations of the Book

There have been three main kinds of interpretation of this book. The first is the *literal*. According to this view, the song is simply a celebration of the delights of married love, concerning the marriage of Solomon to a young woman called the Shulamite (6:13). The second is the *allegorical* interpretation. According to this view, nothing in the song is to be taken literally, but every detail is to be spiritualized, referring to the love of God for Israel or of Christ for the Church. This view does not permit any historical setting for the song. The third is the *typical* interpretation. This interpretation, in some respects a combination of the other two, is in the opinion of the present writer the correct one. The song does have a literal, historical setting, describing the love of Solomon and the Shulamite. The details belong to this literal series of events. The earthly love of the bridegroom and the bride, however, is a type or divinely appointed prophetic symbol of the love of Christ and the Church.

Here is God's presentation of true and holy married

love as distinguished on the one hand from the false system of asceticism (that which views everything earthly and physical as evil) and the equally false immorality and promiscuity of the world. God ordained marriage before the fall of man (Genesis 1:27, 28; 2:23-25). The New Testament reveals that the very marriage relationship was designed by God to be a picture of the relationship of Christ and the Church (Ephesians 5:22-33; note especially verse 32; compare Hebrews 13:4).

2. "A Song Which Grace Alone Can Teach . . ."

The song is one lyric poem, consisting mainly of reminiscences of the bridegroom and the bride as they think of their meeting, their courtship and subsequent marriage. The story is told by means of dialogue and is difficult to follow. However, through the terms of address, one can usually detect which person is speaking. The bridegroom invariably calls the bride "my love," while she refers to him as "my beloved." Certain lines are spoken by a group called the daughters of Jerusalem. As Hudson Taylor said, "This is a song which grace alone can teach and experience alone can learn."[1]

What reverent and believing person can doubt that above and beyond the earthly bridegroom can be seen the features of the heavenly Bridegroom Himself, the One who is indeed "altogether lovely"? (5:16). To belong to Christ through faith in Him is to be a member of His body which is mysteriously and wonderfully also His bride.

---

[1] J. Hudson Taylor, *Union and Communion* (London: Morgan and Scott).

Self Check Test 8

Check up on what you know about the books of Solomon. (See page 165 for instructions.)

In the right-hand column circle the following statements "true" or "false":

1. Solomon wrote three books of the Old Testament. (p. 191)   T   F

2. In the original Hebrew the verses in Proverbs which describe the virtuous woman are alphabetical. (p. 193)   T   F

3. The book of Ecclesiastes shows that philosophy can solve most problems. (p. 194)   T   F

4. Solomon wrote 105 songs. (p. 196)   T   F

5. God is directly mentioned five times in The Song of Solomon. (p. 196)   T   F

6. The typical interpretation of The Song of Solomon combines much of the literal and allegorical interpretations. (p. 196)   T   F

7. The bridegroom invariably calls the bride "my love" in The Song of Solomon. (p. 197)   T   F

8. The bride invariably calls the bridegroom "my beloved" in The Song of Solomon. (p. 197)   T   F

9. Beyond the earthly bridegroom in The Song of Solomon can be seen the features of the Lord Himself. (p. 197)   T   F

10. The Song of Solomon was written by King Lemuel. (p. 196)   T   F

Circle the letter of the correct statement.

11. The Proverbs were
    a. all written by Solomon.
    b. all collected by Solomon.
    c. principally written by Solomon.
    d. all written by King Hezekiah (p. 191).

12. In the New Testament, wisdom is
    a. found in Christ.
    b. described as "the fear of the LORD."
    c. intellectual knowledge.
    d. not discussed at all (p. 192).

Dig Deeper in Your Bible

13. The following chart gives places in Ecclesiastes where the expression "under the sun" and the similar expressions, "under heaven" and "on (or upon) the earth," occur. Complete the chart by filling in the verse number opposite each unfinished chapter reference. (Note: Not all of these expressions are necessarily listed on the chart since, in some cases, they occur more than once in a given verse.)

1:3	1:	1:13	2:	2:	2:	2:
2:	2:	3:1	3:	4:	4:	4:
4:	5:2	5:	5:	6:	6:	8:
8:14	8:	8:16	8:	9:	9:	9:
9:	9:	9:	10:	10:7	11:2	11:3

Turn to page 309 to find the correct answers.

Do not send the answers to the Correspondence School.

Lesson 16

Introduction to the Prophetical Books

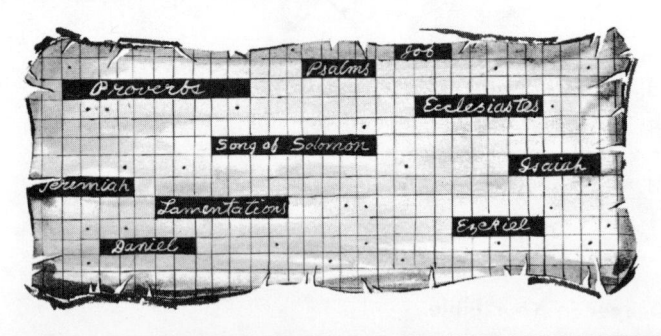

THE WRITING PROPHETS			
Century	*Pre-exilic*	*Exilic*	*Postexilic*
B.C. 9th	Obadiah Joel Jonah		
8th	Amos Hosea ISAIAH Micah		
7th	Nahum Zephaniah Habakkuk JEREMIAH	EZEKIEL DANIEL	
6th			Haggai Zechariah
5th			Malachi

The books from Isaiah through Malachi are generally spoken as of the prophetical books. When the term *prophecy* is used, most of us think of prediction of the future. This has come to be the common use of the word, but it was not its original meaning. A prophet in the Scripture is someone whom God has raised up especially in a time of unbelief and apostasy to be an official spokesman for Him. The prophet gives forth God's message.

In this respect the office of prophet differs from that of priest. Note the following diagram:

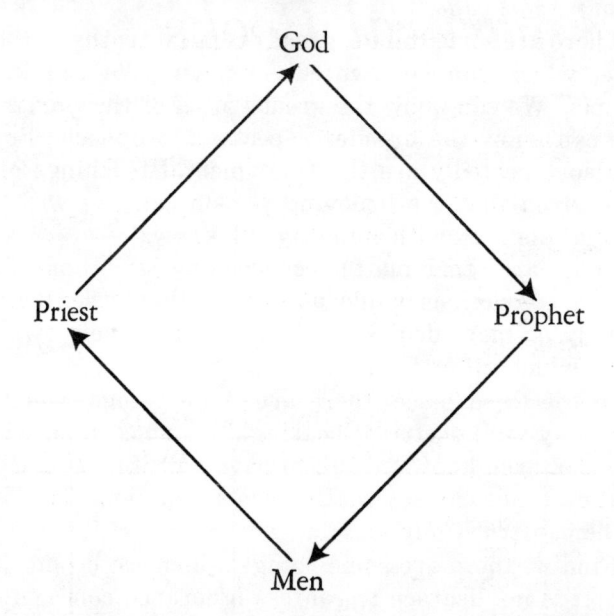

```
                    God
                   ↗   ↘
                  ↙     ↘
            Priest       Prophet
                  ↖     ↙
                   ↘   ↙
                    Men
```

A priest represents men before God. A prophet represents God before men. Sometimes the same person was called by God to be both priest and prophet (for example, Jeremiah and Ezekiel), but the two offices were usually distinct.

As a part of his message from God, the prophet frequently was instructed by God concerning the future. This prediction of future events was a sign and guarantee of the truthfulness of the prophet's message, his credential as being truly God's messenger.

There were prophets in all periods of Israel's history, but the prophetic office came into greater prominence after the division of the kingdom, particularly as first Israel and then Judah began to decline spiritually and morally. Consistent failure, both in the priesthood and in the kingship, resulted in a greater use by God of prophets.

DIFFERENT DEGREES OF KNOWLEDGE

When we face the prophetic portion of the Word of God, especially the predictive prophecies, we find many things which are difficult to interpret. In connection with the Bible generally, we need to recognize at least *four different degrees of our knowledge.*

There are some things, great essential truths of the Scripture, which can be assuredly known. We can know the Gospel. We can know the great truths of the Christian life. We can know the broader aspects of prophecy. So clearly and so repeatedly are the fundamental teachings of Scripture given that the believing person can say with thanksgiving, and yet with humility, "I know."

There are other matters concerning which one can have strong convictions while admitting that other Christians, equally or more dedicated than he, have their own convictions which differ from his.

In the third place, there are those things which do not have any vital doctrinal bearing, and concerning which one does not even know enough to have a definite conviction. In that case, one can say that he has an opinion. This is as far as he can truthfully go.

Finally, there are some things which we do not know at all. It is no disgrace to confess ignorance concerning some details in the Scriptures. The fact that the Bible is God's Word guarantees that there will be much in it that is beyond our comprehension. This is no ground either for discouragement or for complacency, but rather for humility and for diligence in study.

THE PURPOSE OF PROPHECY

In the realm of prophetic study much damage has undoubtedly been done to the cause of the Lord Jesus Christ by cocksureness of many students about details of future events. We must learn to be cautious in our interpretation and not to read into the Scripture things that are not actually there.

Furthermore, we must not think of prophecy as some sort

of glorified jigsaw puzzle in which we fit the pieces together merely for intellectual stimulation. The study of prophecy is presented in the Scripture as a practical, life-affecting matter. All prophecy points either directly or indirectly toward the Lord Jesus Christ. "The testimony of Jesus is the spirit of prophecy" (Revelation 19:10). Its effect should be, not merely to help us understand God's plan for the future, although that is certainly important, but to make our lives better here and now. The Scripture says, "Every man that hath this hope in him purifieth himself, even as he is pure" (I John 3:3).

THE WRITING PROPHETS

From Isaiah through Malachi there are seventeen books written by sixteen different prophets. (The book of Lamentations was written by Jeremiah.) These Old Testament prophets range in date from the middle of the ninth century (about 850 B.C.) until near the end of the fifth century (about 425 B.C.). The ninth century saw the ministries of the great prophets, Elijah and Elisha, recorded in I and II Kings. These men, however, left no writing (with the exception of one letter from Elijah the prophet to King Jehoram of Judah, recorded in II Chronicles 21:12-15).

The writing prophets are usually divided into three groups, according to their relationship to the Babylonian captivity. Those who ministered before the captivity are spoken of as the pre-exilic prophets; those who ministered during the captivity, as the exilic prophets; and those who ministered after the captivity, as the postexilic prophets.

Often the beginning student of Scripture will have great difficulty in distinguishing among these prophets. At first it will seem, because of his unfamiliarity with the various names, that there are many more than there actually are. As a matter of fact, there are eleven pre-exilic prophets, two exilic, and three postexilic. The student might do well to consider these groups in reverse order for convenience, since the three postexilic prophets are easily remembered. They wrote the last three books in the Old Testament: Haggai, Zechariah and Malachi. Furthermore, the two great prophets of the Exile are well known: Ezekiel and Daniel. Most of the difficulties arise in connection with the eleven pre-exilic prophets.

Here too, however, some of the difficulties are more apparent than real, for there are two great clusters of prophets: one in the eighth century B.C. and the other in the seventh. These two groups center respectively around the two well-known prophets, Isaiah and Jeremiah, with four prophets in each group.

The four prophets in the eighth-century group are, in chronological order, Amos, Hosea, Isaiah, and Micah. The first two of these had their ministry primarily to the Kingdom of Israel. (Although Amos was a native of Judah, he was sent by God to Israel to prophesy.) The last two ministered primarily to Judah. We need not speculate concerning the relative time of the prophets, since each of them mentions the kings during whose reigns he prophesied.

In the time of the prophets of the seventh century, of course, only the Kingdom of Judah was still in existence, since Israel was destroyed as a nation by the Assyrians in 722 B.C. Jeremiah prophesied during the last forty years of the Kingdom of Judah. The prophet Nahum was earlier, about the middle of the seventh century; Zephaniah and Habakkuk were contemporaries, at least during the early years of Jeremiah's ministry.

This accounts for all except three of the writing prophets. The dates of these—Obadiah, Joel, and Jonah—are somewhat harder to establish, since they do not mention the king in whose reign they prophesied. It is possible, however, by comparison with a reference to Jonah in II Kings 14:25, to see that Jonah lived and ministered either before the reign of Jeroboam II of Israel or early in his reign. This would place him approximately around the year 800 B.C. or slightly later. Joel was perhaps as early as 825 B.C. The reason concerning this is somewhat more involved, and will be discussed in Lesson 21. Obadiah is the most difficult of the prophets to be placed chronologically. Even conservative scholars have differed by as much as almost three centuries, some placing him first of all, around 850 B.C.; others putting him in the time of Jeremiah, shortly after the destruction of

Jerusalem by the Babylonians in 586 B.C. This survey adopts the early date for Obadiah. The reasons are given in Lesson 22.

The student should familiarize himself with the prophets in a general way, seeing their relationships to one another before attempting to consider the details of the individual prophecies.

HISTORICAL BACKGROUND OF THE PROPHETS

As has been mentioned in Part I, Lesson 10, of this survey, II Kings gives the historical background for the writing prophets. As someone has said, what the book of Acts is to the epistles in the New Testament, II Kings is to the prophets in the Old Testament. A knowledge of the factual content of II Kings will help immeasurably in the understanding of the prophetical books.

The prophets were often lonely men, men who had to take a stand for God in the midst of unbelievers and scoffers, frequently risking their lives to give the testimony which God required of them. The New Testament says, "Take, my brethren, the prophets, who have spoken in the name of the Lord, for an example of suffering affliction, and of patience" (James 5:10).

Peter tells us that the prophets searched their own writings diligently, seeking to discover the meaning of many of the wonderful truths God revealed to them. In I Peter 1:10-12 we read, concerning the message of salvation, which God revealed through the prophets: "Of which salvation the prophets have inquired and searched diligently, who prophesied of the grace that should come unto you: searching what, or what manner of time the Spirit of Christ which was in them did signify, when [he] . . . testified beforehand the sufferings of Christ, and the glory that should follow. Unto whom it was revealed, that not unto themselves, but unto us they did minister the things, which are now reported unto you by them that have preached the Gospel unto you with the Holy Ghost sent down from heaven; which things the angels desire to look into."

Thus we see that the great theme of the prophets' messages is the Lord Jesus Christ in His first and second advents. The prophets themselves did not know of the long interval between the two comings of the Messiah, and were often perplexed at the blending of prophecies concerning Christ's glory with prophecies concerning His suffering. The New Testament is for us the key to the interpretation of the Old Testament prophecies. May we see clearly in the pages of Scripture the One whom the prophets often saw only dimly, far in the future—the Lord Jesus Christ, the Son of God.

Survey of the Scriptures
A Moody Correspondence Course

Exam 8
Lessons 15, 16

Name_____
(Print plainly)

Exam Grade_____

Address_____ Date_____

City_____ State_____ Zip Code_____ Class Number_____

Instructor_____

**LESSON 15   PROVERBS—ECCLESIASTES
            THE SONG OF SOLOMON**

In the blank space write the letter of the correct or most nearly correct answer.

1. "Ecclesiastes" means

    a. "the prophet."
    b. "the priest."
    c. "the king."
    d. "the preacher."   _____

2. Ecclesiastes teaches that life lived "under the sun" without reference to God is

    a. satisfying.
    b. futile.
    c. worthwhile if a person works hard.
    d. all right while a person is young.   _____

3. The Song of Solomon depicts

    a. the relationship between Christ and His own.
    b. the need for asceticism.
    c. the pleasures of immorality.
    d. the pitfalls of marriage.   _____

207

4. Each of the following phrases can be described as (1) empiricism or (2) rationalism. Indicate the correct answer by writing (1) or (2) in the blank space.

   a. the **only** valid knowledge comes through reasoning　_____

   b. depending on the senses for knowledge　_____

   c. Solomon's repeated expression, "I saw"　_____

   d. "I said in mine heart"　_____

5. What verse in the New Testament is given in this lesson to show the inadequacy of both empiricism and rationalism as methods of fathoming ultimate truths?　_____

Use Your Bible

You may use your Bible to answer questions 6 and 7.

6. Give the reference and write out one proverb which deals with the subject of parental chastening of children.

   _____

   _____

   _____

   _____

   _____

7. Give the Scripture reference for one passage in The Song of Solomon which describes the bridegroom as being "altogether lovely."

   _____

8. What grounds are suggested in the textbook for the belief that Solomon was the author of Ecclesiastes?

   _____

   _____

   _____

9. a. Chapters 1—9 of Proverbs is a contrast of

   _____

   and _____

   b. The purpose of the book of Proverbs is to

   _____

   c. In which chapter of Proverbs do we find the description of the virtuous woman?

   _____

   d. Which of the poetic books is read annually at the Passover?

   _____

   e. The three interpretations of the Song of Solomon are the allegorical, the typical and the literal interpretations. Which of these interpretations is regarded by the author of this course to be the correct one?

   _____

10. The proverbs are meant to be a guide to your daily life as the psalms are to your devotional life. This question is designed to help you see how the proverbs illuminate the lives of people.

Each of the following proverbs can be applied to one of the Bible characters listed below. Read the stories in the Scripture verses given in a to e below and write the chapter and verse of the appropriate proverb in the blank space.

Proverbs 1:7	". . . fools despise wisdom and instruction."
Proverbs 1:10	"My son, if sinners entice thee, consent thou not."
Proverbs 12:10	". . . the tender mercies of the wicked are cruel."
Proverbs 17:5	". . . he that is glad at calamities shall not be unpunished."
Proverbs 26:27	"Whoso diggeth a pit shall fall therein."

a. Joseph   Genesis 39:1-10   _____

b. Haman   Esther 7:10   _____

c. Shimei   II Samuel 16:5-8

                I Kings 2:1, 8, 9, 36-46   _____

d. Pilate   Luke 23:13-16   _____

e. Rehoboam   I Kings 12:1-19   _____

LESSON 16 INTRODUCTION TO THE PROPHETICAL BOOKS

In the blank space at the right-hand margin write "True" or "False" after each of the following statements:

11. The study of prophecy should have a practical effect on our lives. _____

12. Amos prophesied mainly to Judah. _____

13. Habakkuk prophesied at an earlier date than Nahum. _____

14. The prophets were very popular. _____

15. Christ's two advents are the great themes of the prophets. _____

16. The prophets always thoroughly understood their own prophecies. _____

17. II Kings gives the historical background for the writing prophets. _____

18. Every Christian can know the fundamental teachings of Scripture. _____

19. It is a disgrace to have to admit that there are some parts of Scripture we cannot understand. _____

In the blank space write the letter of the correct or most nearly correct answer.

20. The offices of priest and prophet were combined in one person
    a. usually.
    b. never.
    c. sometimes.
    d. always.   _____

21. Prophets were usually raised up in Israel's history in times of

   a. religious revival.
   b. moral awakening.
   c. national expansion.
   d. deepening apostasy.

22. Elisha was

   a. not a prophet.
   b. the prophet who wrote to King Jehoram.
   c. a non-writing prophet.
   d. the last of the prophets.

23. By "the Exile" is meant

   a. the time Israel spent in bondage in Egypt.
   b. the Assyrian captivity.
   c. the present dispersal of the Jews.
   d. the Babylonian captivity.

24. At the time of the prophets of the seventh century

   a. only Judah was still in existence.
   b. only Israel was still in existence.
   c. Israel and Judah were both in existence.
   d. Israel and Judah had been reunited.

25. The most difficult of the prophets to place chronologically is

   a. Hosea.
   b. Malachi.
   c. Obadiah.
   d. Jonah.

26. Name the missing prophets represented on the chart by the following letters:

a. _____

b. _____

c. _____

d. _____

e. _____

Century B.C.	THE WRITING PROPHETS		
	Pre-exilic	Exilic	Postexilic
9th	Obadiah Joel A		
8th	B Hosea ISAIAH Micah		
7th	C Zephaniah D JEREMIAH		
6th		EZEKIEL DANIEL	Haggai E
5th			Malachi

Use Your Bible

You may use your Bible to complete this exam.

27. Glance through the opening chapter of each of the prophetic books, and in the blank spaces name the prophets who ministered at the time the following kings reigned. Restrict your answer to the one prophet who dates his prophecies by specifically mentioning the king or kings listed in each case.

a. Josiah, king of Judah _____

b. Uzziah, Jotham, Ahaz and Hezekiah, kings of Judah; and Jeroboam, the son of Joash, king of Israel _____

c. the second year of Darius _____

d. the fifth year of King Jehoiachin's captivity _____

Reading Chart

Check (X) the chapters you have read.

PROVERBS					5				10
			15			20			25
			30						
ECCLESIASTES					5				10
SONG OF SOLOMON					5				

——————————————————MAIL TO ADDRESS ON BACK COVER.

Lesson 17

Isaiah

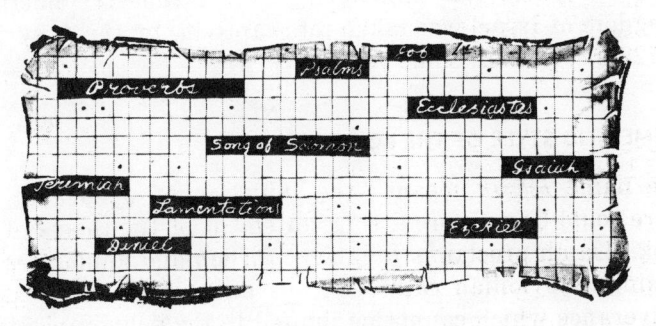

Judah	Prophets	Israel	World Powers
Uzziah		Jeroboam II	
		Zachariah	
		Shallum	
		Menahem	• Israel "buys off" Assyria
		Pekahiah	
	—|740 B.C.		
Jotham		Pekah	• 2½ tribes east of Jordan taken captive by Assyria
Ahaz			
			• Samaria besieged by Assyrians
	ISAIAH	Hoshea	• Northern Kingdom falls and Assyrian captivity begins 722 B.C.
Hezekiah		Assyrian captivity	
			• Assyrians invade Judah God intervenes to save Jerusalem
Manasseh			
II Kings 15—20	Isaiah 1:1; 36—39	II Kings 14—17	

The book of Isaiah receives its name from the writer, "Isaiah the son of Amoz" (1:1). The prophet's ministry continued during the reigns of four kings of Judah: Uzziah, Jotham, Ahaz, and Hezekiah, although he did not begin his work until almost the end of Uzziah's reign. Consequently, he must have had a ministry of about forty years. This would be during the latter half of the eighth century B.C. He tells us that he saw the Lord in the year that King Uzziah died (740 B.C.). He was ministering at the time the northern Kingdom of Israel was taken into captivity by the Assyrians in 722 B.C. and for some years after that.

THEME AND STYLE OF THE BOOK

The name *Isaiah* means "the salvation of Jehovah," and there could be no more fitting statement of the theme of the book. Isaiah proclaims judgment for sin and announces the coming Babylonian captivity, but he goes on to speak of deliverance which cannot be limited to the deliverance from Babylon under Cyrus, prominent as that is in the book. A far greater deliverance is in view, deliverance by the Messiah, Immanuel; the extension of Jehovah's salvation through His Servant to the "ends of the earth"; the worldwide rule of Christ in righteousness and peace.

Large portions of the book of Isaiah are poetic. Figures of speech abound. In extent and variety of vocabulary, Isaiah excels. Play on words and alliteration are prominent, but are not usually evident in the English translation. The use of a refrain is a frequent literary device which can be carried over into the English. There are a number of songs in the book, for example, the song of the vineyard (chapter 5), the song of the coming salvation (chapter 12), the song of the rejoicing desert (chapter 35), the song of the restored wife (chapter 54).

ISAIAH, THE PROPHET OF THE GOSPEL

No book of the Old Testament, except Psalms, is quoted or referred to in the New Testament as often as Isaiah. Isaiah is frequently called the evangelical prophet, the prophet of the Gospel. This book abounds in references to the coming Saviour. One could reconstruct a fairly detailed account of the earthly life and ministry, the death and resurrection of the Lord Jesus Christ from the pages of Isaiah. These Messianic references are not confined to one section of the book, but are scattered all through it. To cite a few examples, this is the book of the virgin-born Immanuel (7:14); of the Child born and Son given whose name is "Wonderful, Counsellor, The mighty God, The everlasting Father, The Prince of Peace" (9:6); of the Branch from the roots of Jesse (11:1); of the King who shall "reign in righteousness" (32:1); of the One who feeds "his flock like a shepherd" (40:11); of the Servant in whom God finds His delight (42:1); of the Man of sorrows and the Lamb brought to the slaughter (53:3, 7). These and others are vivid pictures of the Lord Jesus Christ written down by inspiration seven hundred years before He came into the world.

As we look through the New Testament, we see in many places the name of Isaiah (Esaias in the Authorized Version, from the Greek spelling of the name). Matthew quotes Isaiah to show that Jesus of Nazareth is the promised Messiah and King (Matthew 4:14; 8:17; 12:17). John the Baptizer, as he begins his mighty ministry, quotes Isaiah (John 1:23). The Lord Jesus Himself in the synagogue at Nazareth reads from the book of Isaiah and announces the fulfillment of the prophecy which He has read (Luke 4:16-21). John reports that Isaiah spoke of the glory of the Lord Jesus (John 12:41). The Ethiopian treasurer, returning home from his trip to Jerusalem, is reading Isaiah (Acts 8:26-33). Paul in both his oral and his written ministry quotes Isaiah (Acts 28:25-27; Romans 9:27, 29; 10:16, 20; 15:12).

HISTORICAL BACKGROUND OF ISAIAH

The historical background of Isaiah is found in II Kings and II Chronicles. The dominant world power in Isaiah's day was Assyria. Before this time Egypt had been very important. Now, however, Egypt's power was ebbing and it became involved in a struggle to the death with the rising, aggressive Assyrian kingdom. This helps one to understand the political allusions in Isaiah. During the prophet's lifetime Assyria swallowed up the northern kingdom, Israel, and invaded the prophet's own country of Judah, seriously threatening it.

Judah was ruled by the descendants of David. Some of these were wicked, some good. Outward prosperity during Uzziah's long reign caused the nation to forget God. Uzziah (also called Azariah) and his son, Jotham, on the whole were good kings in spite of Uzziah's attempt late in life to intrude into the priest's office (II Kings 15:3, 34; II Chronicles 26:16-21).

Jotham's son, Ahaz, was an evil man who introduced

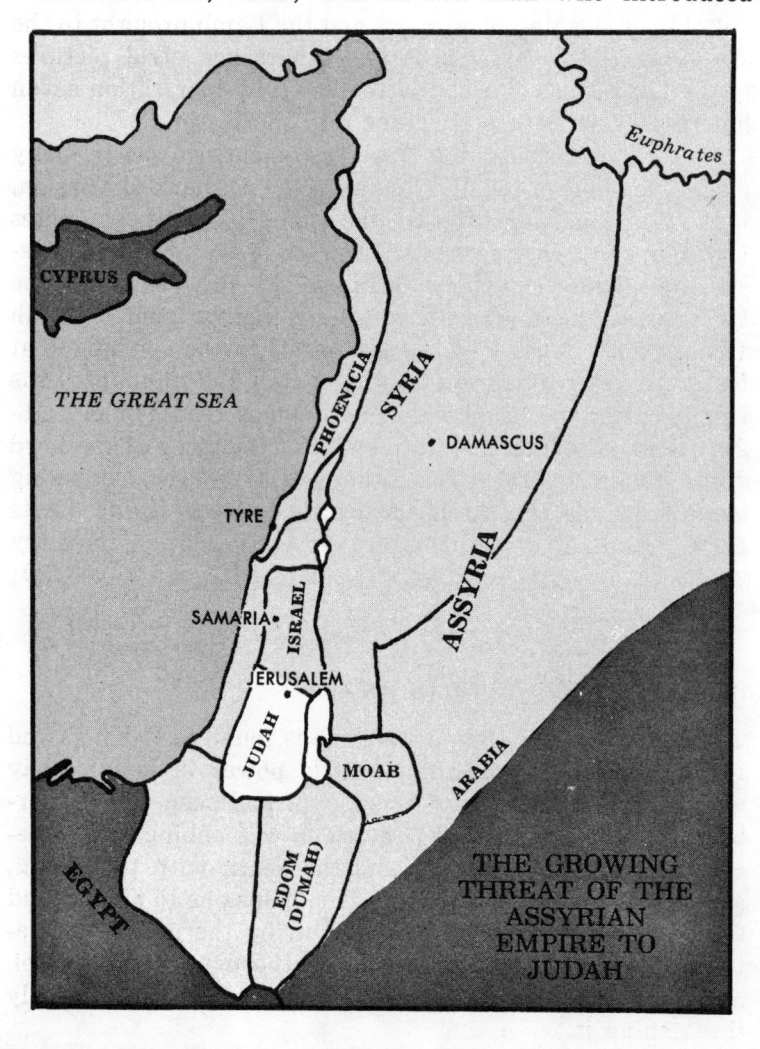

THE GROWING THREAT OF THE ASSYRIAN EMPIRE TO JUDAH

abominable pagan practices into Judah (II Kings 16:2-4). At various times Judah sought alliances either with Assyria or with Egypt. Isaiah denounced these alliances and called upon the nation to turn back to God. In the distance loomed the Babylonian captivity, the theme of much of Isaiah's prophecy, although the new Babylonian Empire had not become powerful in Isaiah's day and did not threaten Judah until a century later, in the time of King Josiah and the prophet Jeremiah.

In spite of the downward spiritual trend, there was revival in Judah for a time under Hezekiah, one of the best and most remarkable of all the kings (II Kings 18:1—20:21; II Chronicles 29:1—32:33). King Hezekiah and the prophet Isaiah were friends and compatriots in a time of danger and apostasy.

STRUCTURE OF THE BOOK

The book of Isaiah is in two main divisions. There is a clear difference between these two parts, so much in fact that destructive critics of the Bible have denied the unity of Isaiah. These critics, of course, have exaggerated the differences and ignored the similarities.

An easy way to remember the divisions of Isaiah is to recall that there are as many chapters in the first part of the book as there are books in the Old Testament (thirty-nine) and as many chapters in the second part of the book as there are books in the New Testament (twenty-seven).

One can say in a general way that the first part of Isaiah has as its theme *judgment from God* and that the second part has as its theme *comfort from God*. The dominant note in each case is struck at the very beginning—God's ringing indictment of the Kingdom of Judah in chapter 1, where the city of Jerusalem is actually called Sodom and Gomorrah (1:10); and in chapter 40 God's call to speak comforting words to Jerusalem after her severe trials (40:1, 2).

The first six chapters come to a climax with Isaiah's account of his vision of the Lord and are further set apart by the time note at the beginning of chapter 7, which introduces a later prophecy. In a similar way chapters 7—12 have a central theme, for the trouble in the time of Ahaz gives occasion to the great prophecy of Immanuel and His coming kingdom. There is no difficulty in recognizing a distinct section in chapters 13—23. Here the unifying word is *burden*, a prophecy of grievous import. Chapters 24—27 likewise form a unity, describing events of the last days. The next section is clearly defined by the use of the word *woe* and includes chapters 28—33. A brief section composed of two chapters (34 and 35) follows, again leading up to the kingdom age. The concluding section in this part of the book tells the historical events in Hezekiah's reign (chapters 36—39). This seems to be a logical grouping of the material in the first part of Isaiah and has the advantage of being based largely upon clues in the text itself. Consequently, we can list the seven sections in the first part of Isaiah as follows:

Part One: The Judgment of God (chapters 1—39)

    I. OPENING PROPHECIES (chapters 1—6)

    II. PROPHECIES OF IMMANUEL (chapters 7—12)

    III. THE BURDENS (chapters 13—23)

    IV. PUNISHMENT AND KINGDOM BLESSING (chapters 24—27)

    V. THE WOES (chapters 28—33)

    VI. INDIGNATION AND GLORY (chapters 34 and 35)

    VII. HISTORICAL INTERLUDE (chapters 36—39)

In the second part of the book, Isaiah looks beyond the Babylonian captivity to the return and sees that return as a foreshadowing of a greater future deliverance through the Messiah. From this ideal point of view the prophet can see the captivity as past (although literally it did not begin until about a century after Isaiah's lifetime) and can rejoice in the glory of God's restoration of Israel.

The twenty-seven chapters in the second part of Isaiah are clearly grouped into three sections of nine chapters each. This is not an arbitrary or whimsical arrangement of commentators, for it is imbedded in the structure of the book itself. Twice in this part of the book God makes the statement, "There is no peace ... unto the wicked." This double utterance marks the threefold division of the second part of Isaiah (48:22; 57:21).

This part of Isaiah seems to be arranged symmetrically. Chapters 40—48 tell of the coming deliverance from Babylon and draw the contrast between the true God and idols. This deliverance is to be brought about by Cyrus, the Persian king, who is mentioned by name in the very heart of the section (44:28; 45:1). Above and beyond the deliverance of the nation from Babylon is the recognition of the greater deliverance through the Messiah, the Lord Jesus Christ.

The omniscient God, through the prophet Isaiah in the eighth century B.C., announces Cyrus as the restorer of the people to Jerusalem. Cyrus did not live until the sixth century B.C. The historical fulfillment of the prophecy is told in II Chronicles 36:22, 23 and Ezra 1:1-11. Cyrus is the only Gentile king who is called God's "anointed."

Chapters 49—57, forming the central section of the second part of Isaiah, have as their main theme the two great lines of Messianic prophecy which are mentioned in the New Testament: "the sufferings of Christ, and the glory that should follow" (I Peter 1:11).

In Isaiah *the nation of Israel* is sometimes called "the servant of Jehovah." Sometimes that designation is used only for *the believing remnant* within the nation and sometimes the term is used for an individual, *the Messiah*. In this section Christ is set forth in His Person and work.

Chapter 53, the heart of this section, gives a wonderful prophetic picture of the suffering and death of the Lord Jesus. The great majority of the quotations from and references to the book of Isaiah in the New Testament are references to this one chapter. When Philip met the Ethiopian treasurer on the desert road and was asked concerning this chapter, "Of whom speaketh the prophet this? of himself, or of some other man?" Philip did not hesitate. The Scripture says, "Then Philip opened his mouth, and began at the same scripture, and preached unto him Jesus" (Acts 8:34, 35).

The closing section, chapters 58—66, brings to a climax the teaching concerning God's purpose for Israel, the coming glory of His people. There is a strong contrast throughout the section between the rebellious and the faithful, a contrast found often in various portions of the Word of God. Chapters 61—63 form the heart of this concluding section. In chapter 61 the Messiah's ministry is described. This is the portion quoted by the Lord in the synagogue at Nazareth. Chapter 62 shows the result of His ministry in Israel's restoration; and chapter 63 announces the day of vengeance of our God.

We can, therefore, outline the second part of Isaiah in this way:

Part Two: The Comfort of God (chapters 40—66)

I. DELIVERANCE OF GOD'S PEOPLE (chapters 40—48)

II. THE SUFFERING SERVANT AS THE REDEEMER (chapters 49—57)

III. THE GLORIOUS CONSUMMATION (chapters 58—66)

Certain impressions can be gained even from a cursory reading of Isaiah. One of these is the magnitude of the prophecy, the wide range of ideas. Another is the reality of the promised kingdom for the nation of Israel. Still another impression is the realization of the majesty and greatness of God. Twenty-five times in the book of Isaiah God is called "the Holy One of Israel." Because He is the Holy One, He can redeem those who put their trust in Him, and He must judge and punish those who reject and disobey Him. Still another outstanding impression already mentioned earlier in the lesson is the Messianic character of the book. We have seen that this is not confined to one section.

But it is not enough to marvel at the prophetic pictures of Christ in Isaiah. One must have a personal relationship to the Christ so described. The gospel is here in its pure essence, given prophetically by the Holy Spirit long before the Lord Jesus actually came into the world. Isaiah saw His glory and we can see His glory, too, in Isaiah's prophecy. God grant that our response may be that of the prophet himself.

"The salvation of Jehovah," the theme of this prophecy, of which the prophet's name is a symbolic testimony, has gone out to the Gentiles. The message of Christ is being proclaimed to "the ends of the earth."

Self-check Test 9

What can you remember about Isaiah?

(See page 165 for instructions.)

In the right-hand column circle the following statements "true" or "false":

1. Isaiah's prophecy concerning a distant coming deliverance has to do simply with the days of Cyrus. (p. 216)   T   F

2. Isaiah is rarely quoted in the New Testament. (p. 216)   T   F

3. A fairly detailed account of Christ's first advent can be gleaned from Isaiah's prophecies. (p. 216)   T   F

4. The last twenty-seven chapters of Isaiah are arranged symmetrically. (p. 221)   T   F

5. A personal relationship to Christ is more important than marveling at the prophetic pictures of Him in Isaiah. (p. 222)   T   F

6. In Isaiah the gospel was given in essence by the Holy Spirit long before Christ came. (pp. 216, 217)   T   F

7. The statement, "There is no peace . . . to the wicked," occurs twice in Isaiah. (p. 221)   T   F

Dig Deeper in Your Bible

Answer the following questions about Part Two of Isaiah by writing the correct chapter numbers in the blank spaces.

    Chapters

8. Which nine chapters are central in Part Two of Isaiah? _____

9. Which chapter of Isaiah is the central chapter of the central nine? _____

10. Which two verses are central in the central chapters of the central nine? _____

11. Which of these two verses was used to bring about the salvation of an important person in the New Testament? _____

Glance through Isaiah 15—23. Then, in the blank spaces, check (√) the Gentile nations listed below which were subjects of Isaiah's prophecy.

12. Egypt _____

13. Moab _____

14. Cyprus _____

15. Arabia _____

16. Tyre _____

Turn to page 309 to find the correct answers.
Please do not send the answers to the Correspondence School.

Lesson 18

Jeremiah and Lamentations

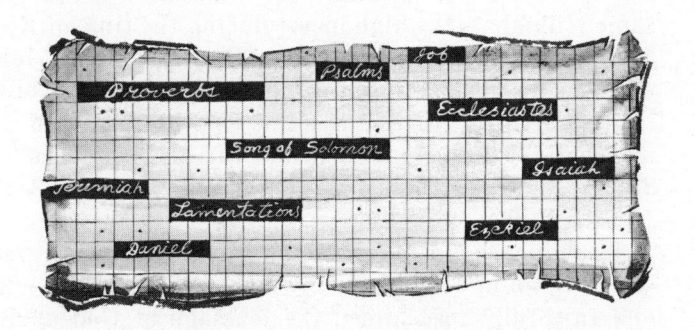

Judah	Prophets	World Powers
Josiah	626 B.C.	
		• Babylon overthrows Assyria
Jehoahaz		
Jehoiakim	JEREMIAH	• 1st Babylonian invasion of Judah
Jehoiachin		• 2nd Babylonian invasion of Judah
Zedekiah		
		• 3rd Babylonian invasion of Judah
Babylonian captivity	?	• Jerusalem taken and temple destroyed Babylonian captivity begins 586 B.C. • Babylon overthrows Egypt
		• Medo-Persia overthrows Babylon
II Kings 23—25 Jeremiah 1:2, 3		

THE BOOK OF JEREMIAH

1. The Writer

This, the longest of the prophetical books, was written by Jeremiah, who was a priest as well as a prophet. His native town was Anathoth, in the tribe-land of Benjamin. This was one of the priestly cities about three miles north of the city of Jerusalem. He identifies himself as the son of Hilkiah; but whether this was the same Hilkiah as the high priest during the time of King Josiah, it is impossible to say. When God called Jeremiah to his prophetic ministry, he was a very young man (1:6). At the command of God he remained unmarried (16:2). He is mentioned in II Chronicles 35: 25; 36:12, 21, 22; Ezra 1:1; Daniel 9:2; Matthew 2:17; 16:14; 27:9.

Jeremiah began his ministry in the thirteenth year of the reign of King Josiah, which was 626 B.C. (1:2), and faithfully proclaimed the message of God during the last forty years of the Kingdom of Judah. He was still prophesying when the city was captured by the Babylonians in the eleventh year of King Zedekiah, or 586 B.C. (1:3).

2. Circumstances of the Book

Jeremiah was the prophet of the decline and fall of the Kingdom of Judah. During the early part of his ministry, before the first Babylonian invasion of the land, Zephaniah and Habakkuk were his contemporaries. During the closing years of his ministry, while he prophesied in Jerusalem, Ezekiel, and Daniel were in the early years of their ministry in the land of Babylon.

As has been mentioned, Jeremiah began his ministry during the reign of Josiah, who was the last great reforming king of Judah. Five years after Jeremiah was called to be a prophet, during the repairing of the temple, "the book of the law," which had been lost for a long period, was rediscovered. This led to repentance on the part of King Josiah and many of the people, and brought about revival in the land.

Josiah was killed by the Egyptians at the battle of Megiddo (II Kings 23:29). His son, Jehoahaz, was proclaimed as king, but reigned only three months before he was deposed by the king of Egypt, whose troops were occupying the land of Judah. Pharaoh (the Egyptian king) set up another son of Josiah, Jehoiakim, as the king of Judah. During the beginning of his reign, Jehoiakim was an Egyptian puppet. But in the third year of his reign the forces of the king of Babylon invaded Judah and during the remainder of his rule, which lasted in its entirety for eleven years, Jehoiakim was subject to the king of Babylon. This *first* Babylonian invasion, mentioned in Daniel 1:1, took place in 606 B.C. Jehoiakim was succeeded by his son, Jehoiachin, who reigned only three months. During this brief period, the Babylonian forces appeared in their *second* invasion of Judah and transported Jehoiachin and many of his people to Babylon. Nebuchadnezzar, the king of Babylon, then set up Zedekiah, another son of Josiah, to be the king. Zedekiah was the last king of Judah. He finally rebelled against the king of Babylon, and the Babylonians came against the land a *third* time, putting the city of Jerusalem under siege and finally capturing it in 586 B.C. (See II Kings 23:31—25:21.)

During a great part of his ministry, Jeremiah was in the strange situation of having to tell his own countrymen to submit to the foreign invader. God's message through him was that Judah must submit to Babylon. From a human point of view, one can see that Jeremiah would be considered by many to be a traitor to his own country. He suffered persecution, both under Jehoiakim and under Zedekiah.

3. Structure of the Book

The prophet's call from God is set forth in chapter 1, which forms an introduction to the prophecy. The bulk of the book contains prophecies against Judah and Jerusalem, foretelling the Babylonian captivity and calling upon Judah to submit to the king of Babylon (chapters 2—45). Following this is a briefer section of prophecies against the nations (chapters 46—51). The book closes with a historical appendix (chapter 52). Therefore, the book may be outlined as follows:

I. INTRODUCTION: THE CALL OF THE PROPHET (chapter 1)

II. PROPHECIES AGAINST JUDAH AND JERUSALEM (chapters 2—45)

III. PROPHECIES AGAINST THE NATIONS (chapters 46—51)

IV. HISTORICAL APPENDIX (chapter 52)

A BRIEF ANALYSIS OF THE BOOK

1. Introduction: The Call of the Prophet (chapter 1)

God called Jeremiah to a very difficult ministry, one in which he would have to face much opposition. His ministry was to be one of tearing down more than of building up (1:10), but God promised to give him courage. In this introduction, describing God's call to Jeremiah, the sign of the almond rod and the seething pot set the keynote of the Babylonian invasion and conquest of Judah. That which Isaiah had seen from afar was now to take place during the lifetime of Jeremiah.

2. Prophecies Against Judah and Jerusalem (chapters 2—45)

The prophecies in the book of Jeremiah are not entirely in chronological order although those in chapters 2—20 seem to have been given mainly during the reigns of Josiah and Jehoiakim. The prophet's message in chapters 2 and 3 reminds Judah of God's love and rebukes the nation for the sin of ingratitude.

The second message (3:6—6:30) warns against the great devastation that is coming from the north. Although Babylon was to the east of Judah, the invasion route was from the north. (See accompanying map.)

In his message at the gate of the Lord's house (7:1—10:25), the prophet warned of a coming exile. In a further message in chapters 11 and 12, he reminded the

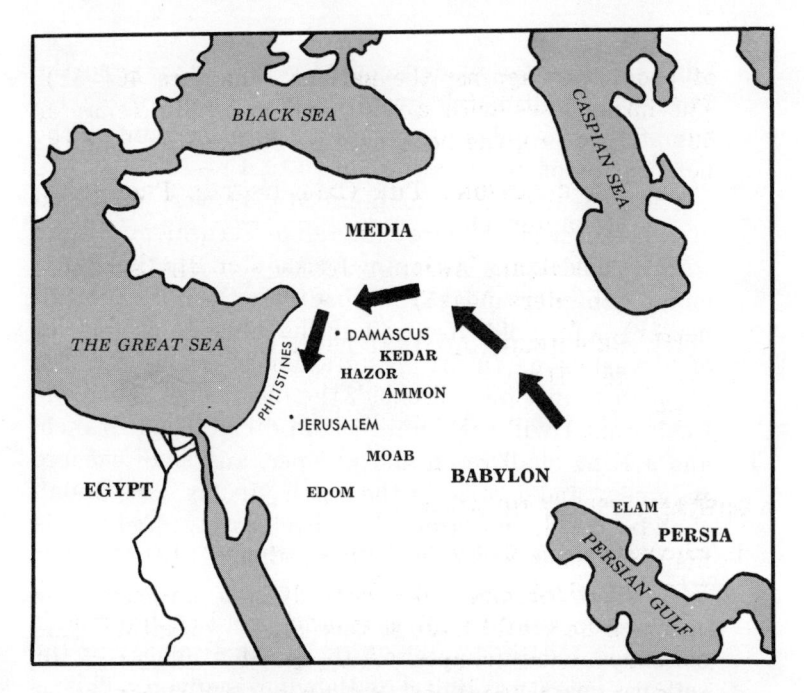

THE NATIONS INCLUDED IN JEREMIAH'S PROPHECY
AND THE "NORTHERN" INVASION

nation of the broken covenant; and in the sign of a linen girdle (chapter 13), he declared that Judah would not be spared even though it had been very close to God. The message on the drought (chapters 14 and 15) reminded the nation that such a natural phenomenon was a sign of judgment from God, as set forth in the Palestinian Covenant, under which Israel entered the land (Deuteronomy 28:23, 24). A message from God concerning Jeremiah's remaining unmarried (16:1—17:18) set Jeremiah as a personal sign to the nation. The prophet's lack of family responsibilities was to call to the attention of the nation the fact that their natural lives were to be disrupted by invasion and captivity. In the message on the Sabbath (17:19-27), God showed how the breaking of His law concerning the Sabbath brings judgment, and is symptomatic of other law-breaking.

In the word concerning the potter's wheel (18:1—19:13), God showed His sovereignty over the nation;

but as the potter made another vessel (18:4), so the Lord would ultimately restore Judah. Before the resumption of prophetic messages, a brief account of the persecution of Jeremiah follows (19:14—20:18).

The messages from chapters 21—39 were delivered at different periods before the fall of Jerusalem. In the word to Zedekiah, beginning in chapter 21, the Babylonian captivity under Nebuchadrezzar (or, Nebuchadnezzar) is foretold. Yet even in the midst of prophecies of devastation, future restoration is seen, and the Messiah is in view. "Behold, the days come, saith the LORD, that I will raise unto David a righteous Branch, and a King shall reign and prosper, and shall execute judgment and justice in the earth. In his days Judah shall be saved, and Israel shall dwell safely: and this is his name whereby he shall be called, THE LORD OUR RIGHTEOUSNESS" (23:5, 6).

Space does not permit a résumé of all of Jeremiah's messages, but in chapter 25 the great prophecy of the seventy years' captivity in Babylon is given. This is undoubtedly the prophecy which Daniel later read (Daniel 9:2).

During a great part of his ministry, Jeremiah endured the opposition of false prophets who tried to give a message of peace when there was no peace, and who claimed that Babylon would never capture the Kingdom of Judah. Even after the deportation of King Jehoiachin and a great multitude of the people, the false prophets were proclaiming that the captivity would be over soon. It was Jeremiah's painful duty to tell the people otherwise; and his letter to those who were already in captivity (chapter 29) contained a message from God, saying that the people were to settle in Babylon because they were to remain there for seventy years.

In chapter 31 God mentioned the New Covenant, referred to later in the New Testament (31:31; compare Hebrews 8:8-12). In a sign of the field which Jeremiah purchased (chapter 32) God showed that, although the land was being invaded and the people were to be deported, yet restoration would come and the land would again be sold. Another great prophecy concerning the kingdom of the Messiah is set forth in chapter 33.

The wicked King Jehoiakim thought that he was destroying part of the Word of God when he cut up the book which the prophet had written and cast the parts into the fire (chapter 36), but God's Word abides.

Jeremiah's imprisonment during the period of the siege of Jerusalem almost led to his death, but his rescue through the kindness of Ebed-melech, the Ethiopian (chapter 38), is set forth with God's commendation of Ebed-melech. The final captivity of Judah is described in chapter 39, and many of the facts are repeated in chapter 52. Prophecies which Jeremiah gave after the fall of Jerusalem are given in chapters 40—45, first to the remnant left in the land, then to the people in Egypt where Jeremiah was forcibly taken. Finally, there is a brief message to Baruch, Jeremiah's friend and secretary (chapter 45).

3. Prophecies Against the Nations (chapters 46—51)

This section contains a number of prophecies against Gentile powers which had been enemies of the people of Israel and Judah. The list begins with Egypt and closes with the greatest enemy of all, Babylon. This mighty and arrogant kingdom which is now taking the people of Judah into captivity will itself, in turn, suffer the judgment of God.

4. Historical Appendix (chapter 52)

The last sentence in 51:64 would seem to indicate that chapter 52 was written by a different person, nevertheless under the inspiration of the Spirit of God. It is a historical résumé, and may be compared with chapter 39 and with II Kings 25:27-30.

THE BOOK OF LAMENTATIONS

This brief poetical book was written by the prophet Jeremiah. As its name indicates, it is a group of dirges or songs of lamentation over the fall of the city of Jerusalem. There are five different songs, and the form is alphabetical. The twenty-two verses in the first Lamentation begin with the twenty-two letters of the Hebrew alphabet in order. This is true also of Lamentations two and four. The third Lamentation has three verses beginning with the first letter of the alphabet, three with the second, and so on throughout the entire alphabet. The fifth Lamentation has twenty-two verses, but for some reason is not alphabetical.

The *first* Lamentation describes the condition of the city after its capture by the Babylonians. It is a condition of wretchedness. The *second* tells us the cause of the overthrow of Zion, or Jerusalem. Her sin has brought the judgment of God upon her. The *third* Lamentation declares God's purpose or design in this affliction. Here, in the middle of the book, we read of God's mercy and faithfulness (3:22, 23). In the *fourth* Lamentation Zion is portrayed as remembering the former days, lamenting the contrast between what she was and what she is now, and describing her enemy. The *fifth* and closing Lamentation contains Zion's pathetic prayer to God, as she pleads her cause with Him. "Turn thou us unto thee, O LORD, and we shall be turned" (5:21).

Throughout these songs we see, not only the sorrow of the prophet Jeremiah, but also the sorrow of God, who did not rejoice in the judgment which He had to bring upon His people, but rather used the judgment as an occasion for an appeal to repentance and trust in Himself.

Survey of the Scriptures
A Moody Correspondence Course

Exam 9
Lessons 17, 18

Name_____ (Print plainly) Exam Grade_____

Address_____ Date_____

City_____ State_____ Zip Code_____ Class Number_____

Instructor_____

LESSON 17   ISAIAH

In the blank space write the letter of the correct or most nearly correct answer.

1. King Ahaz was
   a. a good man, on the whole.
   b. an evil man who introduced abominable idolatry into Judah.
   c. the leader in a great national revival.
   d. a leper.   _____

2. The aggressive world power of Isaiah's day was
   a. Babylon.
   b. Syria.
   c. Assyria.
   d. Egypt.   _____

3. Give two specific instances with Scripture references where Isaiah is quoted in the New Testament.

   a. _____

   _____

   b. _____

   _____

233

4. Name the kings or event indicated on this chart by the following letters:

a. _____

b. _____

c. _____

_____

_____

Judah	Prophets	Israel	World Powers
		Jeroboam II	
	A	Zachariah	
		Shallum	
		Menahem	• Israel "buys off" Assyria
		Pekahiah	
Jotham	740 B.C.	Pekah	• C
Ahaz			
	ISAIAH	Hoshea	• Samaria besieged by Assyrians
	B		• Northern Kingdom falls and Assyrian captivity begins 722 B.C.
		Assyrian captivity	• Assyrians invade Judah God intervenes to save Jerusalem
Manasseh			

Use Your Bible

You may use your Bible to complete the next question.

5. Glance through the chapters in Isaiah's prophecy which give his "burdens" against Gentile nations. Then identify the nations or cities represented on the map below by writing the name of each nation or city beside the correct letter.

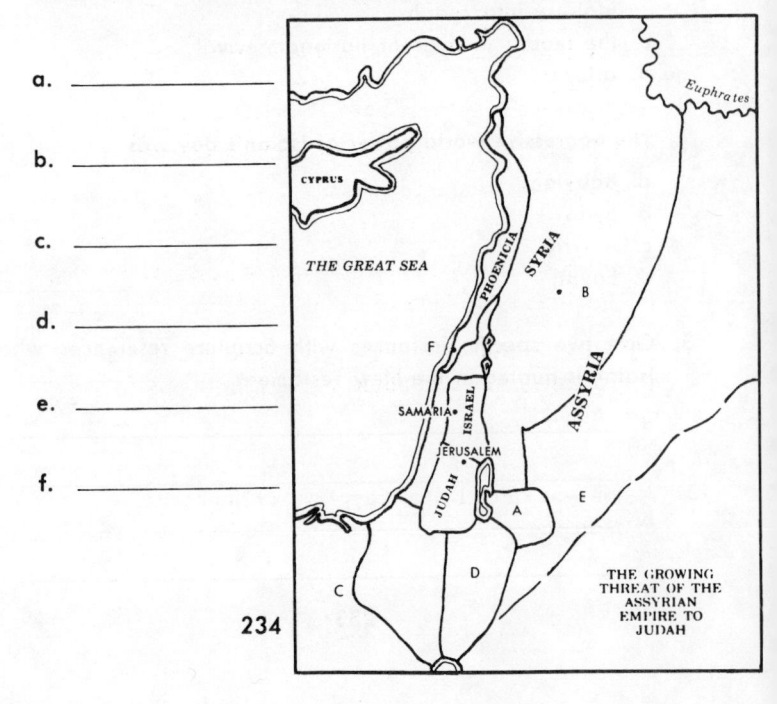

a. _____

b. _____

c. _____

d. _____

e. _____

f. _____

THE GROWING THREAT OF THE ASSYRIAN EMPIRE TO JUDAH

LESSON 18   JEREMIAH AND LAMENTATIONS

In the blank space at the right-hand margin write "True" or "False" after each of the following statements:

6. Many Jews looked upon Jeremiah as a traitor to his country. _____

7. One of the signs given to Jeremiah at his call was the sign of the fig tree. _____

8. With the sign of the girdle Jeremiah warned his people that their past nearness to God would not save them. _____

9. The message of the potter had to do with divine sovereignty. _____

10. The king who destroyed part of the Word of God was Zedekiah. _____

11. Jeremiah is the longest book in the Bible. _____

12. Jeremiah was a married man. _____

13. Jeremiah's ministry began during the reign of the last reforming king of Judah. _____

14. The great enemy of Judah in Jeremiah's day was Assyria. _____

15. Josiah was killed by the Egyptians at the battle of Marenga. _____

In the blank space write the letter of the correct or most nearly correct answer.

16. Jeremiah began his ministry during the reign of
    a. Jehoahaz.
    b. Jehoiachin.
    c. Jehoiakim.
    d. Josiah. _____

17. Jeremiah's early ministry was contemporary with that of
    a. Zechariah and Malachi.
    b. Zephaniah and Habakkuk.
    c. Ezekiel and Daniel.
    d. Amos and Obadiah. _____

18. Jeremiah's closing days in Jerusalem coincided with the ministry, in Babylon, of
    a. Ezekiel and Daniel.
    b. Jonah and Nahum.
    c. Isaiah and Micah.
    d. Joel and Job. _____

19. Jeremiah suffered persecution under
    a. Jehoiakim and Zedekiah.
    b. Jehoiachin and Jehoiakim.
    c. Josiah and Zedekiah.
    d. Jehoahaz. _____

20. Indicate with arrows on this map why Jeremiah warned of a northern invasion, although the nation of Babylon was actually east of Judah and Jerusalem.

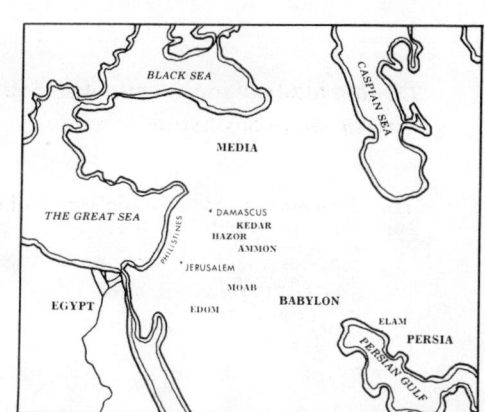

21. Name the kings or events indicated on this chart by the following letters:

a. _____

b. _____

c. _____

d. _____
   _____

e. _____
   _____

Judah	Prophets	World Powers
A	626 B.C.	• Babylon overthrows Assyria
Jehoahaz		
B	JEREMIAH	• 1st Babylonian invasion of Judah
Jehoiachin		• 2nd Babylonian invasion of Judah
C		
		• D
Babylonian captivity	?	• Jerusalem taken and temple destroyed Babylonian captivity begins 586 B.C.
		• E
		• Medo-Persia overthrows Babylon

22. *Complete the following summary of Lamentations:*

Chapters

I. The condition of _____ after
   _____ 1

II. The cause of the overthrow of _____ 2

III. God's _____ 3

IV. Contrasts. The enemy described. 4

V. Zion's _____ 5

23. In the blank space write the chapter number of Lamentations not alphabetical in form: _____

24. Against which of the following nations did Jeremiah not prophesy in that section of his book devoted to prophecies against Gentile powers? Check (√) the correct space or spaces.

Egypt_____ Moab_____ Babylon_____ Persia_____ Elam_____

Reading Chart

Check (×) the chapters you have read.

ISAIAH				5			10
			15		20		25
			30		35		40
			45		50		55
			60		65		
JEREMIAH				5			10
			15		20		25
			30		35		40
			45		50		
LAMENTATIONS				5			

_____MAIL TO ADDRESS ON BACK COVER.

Lesson 19

Ezekiel

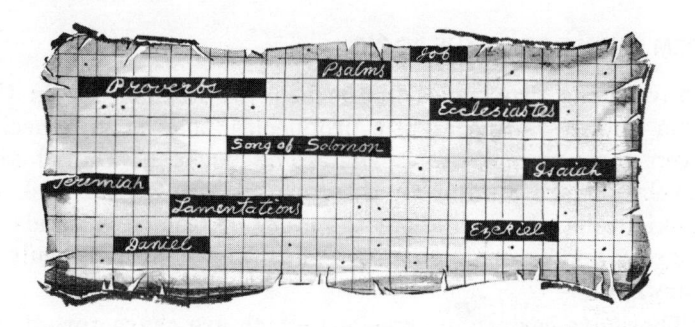

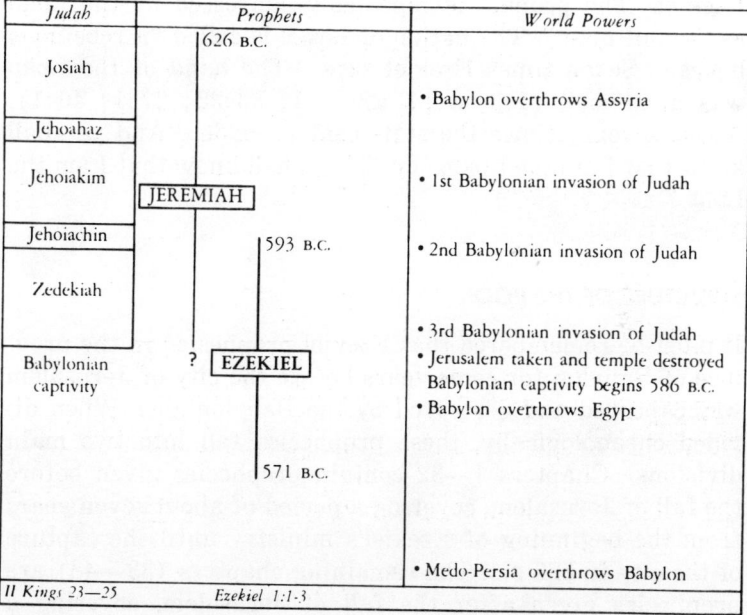

Judah	Prophets	World Powers
Josiah	626 B.C.	
		• Babylon overthrows Assyria
Jehoahaz		
Jehoiakim	JEREMIAH	• 1st Babylonian invasion of Judah
Jehoiachin	593 B.C.	• 2nd Babylonian invasion of Judah
Zedekiah		
		• 3rd Babylonian invasion of Judah
Babylonian captivity	? EZEKIEL	• Jerusalem taken and temple destroyed Babylonian captivity begins 586 B.C. • Babylon overthrows Egypt
	571 B.C.	
		• Medo-Persia overthrows Babylon
II Kings 23—25	Ezekiel 1:1-3	

Ezekiel was among the multitude taken into captivity along with King Jehoiachin in 597 B.C. In the fifth year of his captivity, when he was thirty years of age (1:1, 2), God called him to be a prophet. Like Jeremiah, who was still prophesying in Jerusalem at that time, Ezekiel was both a prophet and a priest. He was probably about the same age as Daniel, who had been taken captive by the Babylonians at an earlier date (606 B.C.). The prophecies in this book cover a period of about twenty-two years.

FORM AND STYLE OF THE BOOK

Many of the prophecies in the book of Ezekiel are in the form known as apocalyptic prophecies, that is, prophecies given through pictorial vision. The books of Daniel and Revelation are similar in this respect. Since the book of Ezekiel tells us much about the glory of God, it abounds in imagery and symbolism, a great deal of which is difficult to understand.

There are certain expressions which are characteristic of Ezekiel. The prophet is repeatedly addressed by the LORD as "son of man." The nation of Israel is called "a rebellious house." Seven times Ezekiel says, "The hand of the LORD was upon me" (1:3; 3:14, 22; 8:1; 33:22; 37:1; 40:1). About seventy times the statement is made, "And ye shall know that I am the LORD," or "They shall know that I am the LORD."

STRUCTURE OF THE BOOK

It must be remembered that Ezekiel prophesied in the province of Babylon for some years before the city of Jerusalem was captured and destroyed by the Babylonians. When divided chronologically, these prophecies fall into two main divisions. Chapters 1—32 contain prophecies given before the fall of Jerusalem, covering a period of about seven years from the beginning of Ezekiel's ministry until the capture of the city in 586 B.C. The remaining chapters (33—48) are prophecies given after the fall of Jerusalem, covering a period of about fifteen years, the latest being dated in the twenty-seventh year of Jehoiachin's captivity, or about 571 B.C. The prophecies in the first division are against Judah (chapters 1—24) and against various Gentile nations (chapters 25—32). The second division describes in graphic detail the new life which God will give to His people, and the new order which He will establish in the land of Israel.

Therefore, the book may be outlined as follows:

I. PROPHECIES GIVEN BEFORE THE FALL OF JERUSALEM (chapters 1—32)
   1. Prophecies Against Judah (chapters 1—24)
   2. Prophecies Against Gentile Nations (chapters 25—32)

II. PROPHECIES GIVEN AFTER THE FALL OF JERUSALEM (chapters 33—48)
   1. Predictions of New Life (chapters 33—37)
   2. Predictions Against Gog and Magog (chapters 38, 39)
   3. Israel in the Kingdom Age (chapters 40—48)

PROPHECIES AGAINST JUDAH

The opening chapters describe the prophet's commissioning by God. The vision which he sees is a manifestation of God's glory, containing many wonderful and inexplicable elements, yet creating an impression of majesty and power. Ezekiel is told by God that he is being sent to a rebellious nation which will not heed His Word (chapter 2). Ezekiel's responsibility, however, is to speak the words of God, whether people listen or not. The eating of the book (chapter 3) denotes the prophet's being filled with the Word of God, that he may give it out to others.

God then proceeds, through various signs, to show the approaching judgment upon Jerusalem (chapters 4 and 5); and following these signs, He gives a clear message about this judgment (chapters 6 and 7).

In chapter 8, the prophet is taken, in vision, to Jerusalem and there permitted to see abominations in the temple which show the necessity of God's judgment. That place which should be the sanctuary of God is being debased and defiled by horrible forms of idolatry. The prophet sees the departure of the glory of the LORD from the Temple because of the sins of the people (11:23).

Not only does God show the necessity of this judgment, but He also shows the absolute certainty of it (chapters 12—19). He will by no means clear Jerusalem. "Though these three men, Noah, Daniel, and Job were in it, they should deliver but their own souls by their righteousness, saith the Lord GOD" (14:14).

In the chapters which follow (20—24) God makes it plain that the sin of Judah is the cause of this judgment. He reminds the nation of His goodness, giving a résumé of His dealings with them and their rebelliousness and hardness of heart (20:1-32). This is followed by a prediction, not only of judgment, but also of another future regathering and restoration to the land, with a judgment upon the nation in that coming day (20:33-44). God announces that there are to be no more kings in Israel until the coming of the Messiah. "I will overturn, overturn, overturn it: and it shall be no more, until he come whose right it is; and I will give it him" (21:27).

There is further rehearsal of Israel's sin (chapter 22). This is reiterated in the parable of Aholah and Aholibah (chapter 23), representing unfaithful Israel and Judah. In the parable of the boiling pot (chapter 24), given by God to the prophet on the day of the beginning of the siege of Jerusalem; and in the death of Ezekiel's wife, the message of certain judgment is emphasized and the prophet is made a sign to the nation. "And thou shalt be a sign unto them; and they shall know that I am the LORD" (24:27).

PROPHECIES AGAINST THE NATIONS

In chapters 25—32, God's visitation of judgment upon surrounding Gentile nations is described. Ammon, Moab, Edom, Philistia, Tyre, Zidon, and Egypt all come into view. In the prophecy against the king of Tyre, there is evidently an allusion to Satan similar to that in the prophecy against the king of Babylon in Isaiah 14. The longest of these prophecies against the nations is that directed against Egypt, which at that time was soon to be conquered by the Babylonians.

PREDICTIONS OF NEW LIFE

God appointed the prophet Ezekiel as the watchman to the house of Israel. In the prophecies given to him after the fall of Jerusalem (33:21), he is seen as one to whom the people listened as they would to a concert, but whose messages were unheeded (33:30-33). The leaders of Israel are addressed as shepherds who are faithless to their responsibilities (chapter 34), but God points forward to the time when He will restore the nation and the Davidic kingdom: "And I will set up one shepherd over them, and he shall feed them, even my servant David; he shall feed them, and he shall be their shepherd" (34:23).

There is much in this section concerning the restoration of the people of Israel and the cleansing of the heart of those who turn to God. For example, 36:25-27 (A.S.V.) is a key passage. There God says: "And I will sprinkle clean water upon you, and ye shall be clean: from all your filthiness, and from all your idols, will I cleanse you. A new heart also will I give you, and a new spirit will I put within you; and I will take away the stony heart out of your flesh, and I will give you a heart of flesh. And I will put my Spirit within you, and cause you to walk in my statutes, and ye shall keep mine ordinances, and do them." It is quite probable that the Lord Jesus Christ had this passage in mind when He exclaimed to Nicodemus, "Art thou a master [the teacher, A:S.V.] of Israel, and knowest not these things?" (John 3:10).

In the vision of the valley of dry bones (chapter 37) there is a vivid picture of the restoration to life of the nation of Israel. (Compare Romans 11:26.)

PREDICTIONS AGAINST GOG AND MAGOG

One of the best known, and yet one of the most difficult prophecies in the book of Ezekiel is that against Gog and Magog (chapters 38 and 39). This is evidently a prophetic reference to a future invasion of the land of Israel from the north, which will take place in the end time.

ISRAEL IN THE KINGDOM AGE

The vision on the Temple and the division of the land (chapters 40—48) has been interpreted in various ways. Some have thought it was fulfilled at the return of those who went back with Zerubbabel (Ezra 1). (*Sheshbazzar*, Ezra 1:8, 11; 5:14, 16, is evidently Zerubbabel's Chaldean name.) However, the temple built in Zerubbabel's day was nothing like the one described in this prophecy. Nor did the glory of the LORD return to that Temple as described in Ezekiel 43. Some interpreters, of course, have declared that the passage is merely idealistic, that it was an imaginary thing, expressing the prophet's dream for his nation. A common interpretation among some conservative Christian scholars is that the passage is allegorical and that it really depicts the Church. The present writer believes that the true interpretation is futuristic and literal, that this is a description of the temple to be built in the millennial age when, according to many other passages of Scripture as well as this one, the nation of Israel will be restored and will be under the rule of the Lord Jesus Christ.

Many details of the prophecy are obscure, but the fact that God will be working is plain and comforting. The climax is reached in the last statement of the book: "And the name of the city from that day shall be, The LORD is there" (48:35). The presence of the Lord Himself will be the chief glory of the Millennium, just as His presence in the life of the individual believer is the sustenance of that life.

Self Check Test 10

Try these questions on Ezekiel.

In the right-hand column circle the following statements "true" or "false":

1. Ezekiel was told to eat a book in order to satisfy his hunger. (p. 241)   T   F

2. Ezekiel saw the glory of the LORD depart from the Temple. (p. 241)   T   F

3. The death of Ezekiel's wife was used as a sign of judgment. (p. 242)   T   F

4. Ezekiel is often spoken of as a "servant of man." (p. 240)   T   F

5. The chief glory of the Millennium will be the holy Temple. (p. 244))   T   F

6. Ezekiel was a priest and king. (pp. 239, 240)   T   F

7. The three righteous men mentioned by Ezekiel were Daniel, Job, and Noah. (p. 242)   T   F

8. Ezekiel's vision of the valley of dry bones pictures the resurrection of Christ. (p. 243)   T   F

9. Gog and Magog are Jewish kings. (p. 243)   T   F

10. Ezekiel went into captivity at the same time as King Jehoiachin. (p. 239)   T   F

Circle the letter of the correct statement.

11. According to the author of this course, the vision of the temple and division of the land

    a. was the result of daydreaming by the prophet.

    b. was fulfilled completely by Zerubbabel.

    c. refers to the Millennium.

    d. is allegorical and points to the Church (pp. 243, 244).

12. Ezekiel began to prophesy in

    a. Babylon before the fall of Jerusalem.

    b. Jerusalem before its fall.

    c. Jerusalem before the fall of Babylon.

    d. Babylon after the fall of Jerusalem (p. 240).

13. Ezekiel's longest prophecy concerning the nations surrounding Jerusalem was addressed to

    a. Ammon.

    b. Moab.

    c. Egypt.

    d. Tyre (p. 242).

Turn to page 309 to find the correct answers.
Please do not send the answers to the Correspondence School.

Lesson 20

Daniel

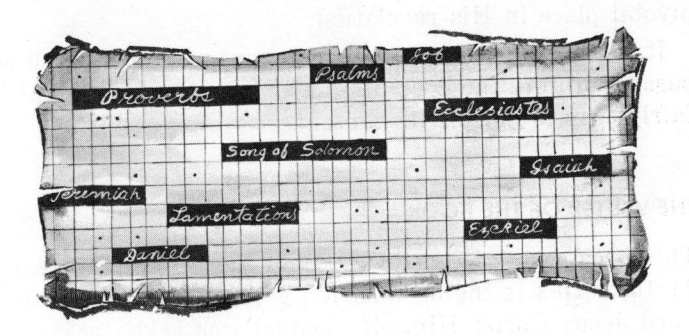

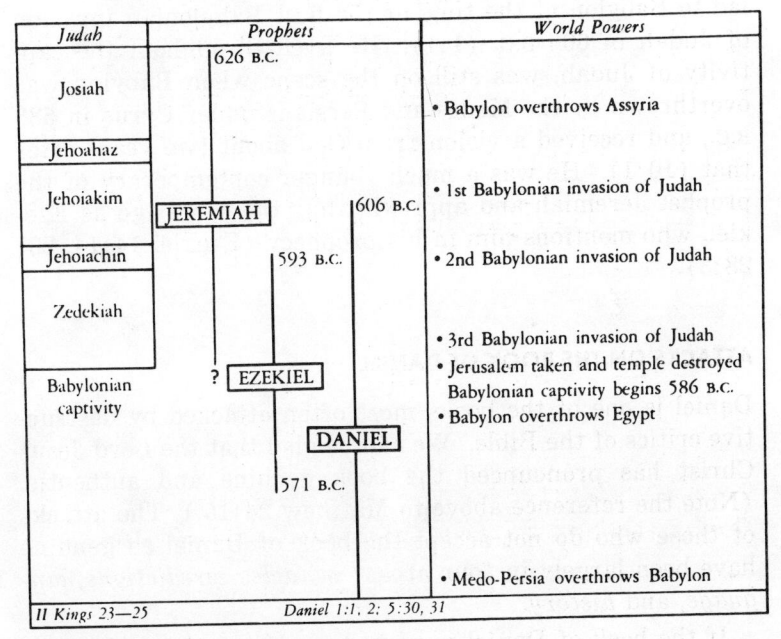

Judah	Prophets		World Powers
	626 B.C.		
Josiah			• Babylon overthrows Assyria
Jehoahaz			
Jehoiakim	JEREMIAH	606 B.C.	• 1st Babylonian invasion of Judah
Jehoiachin		593 B.C.	• 2nd Babylonian invasion of Judah
Zedekiah			
Babylonian captivity	? EZEKIEL		• 3rd Babylonian invasion of Judah • Jerusalem taken and temple destroyed Babylonian captivity begins 586 B.C. • Babylon overthrows Egypt
	DANIEL	571 B.C.	
			• Medo-Persia overthrows Babylon
II Kings 23—25	Daniel 1:1, 2; 5:30, 31		

THE IMPORTANCE OF DANIEL

The book of Daniel is the key to future world events. It is the framework into which other prophecies of the Scriptures fit, and it is essential to the interpretation of other prophetic books, especially the book of Revelation.

Nowhere else in the Word of God do we find so much significant prophecy in such small compass. While we recognize all parts of the Bible as equally inspired, we nevertheless can see that God has given to the book of Daniel a pivotal place in His revelation.

It is a blessing that so much is given in such small compass; therefore the book of Daniel is brief enough that it is fairly easy to master its contents.

THE WRITER OF THE BOOK

This book was written by "Daniel the prophet" (Matthew 24:15). This is the designation given to the writer by the Lord Jesus Christ Himself. Daniel was taken as a young lad to Babylon at the time of the first Babylonian invasion of Judah in 606 B.C. (1:1). He lived throughout the captivity of Judah, was still on the scene when Babylon was overthrown by the Medes and Persians under Cyrus in 539 B.C., and received a vision from God about two years after that (10:1). He was a much younger contemporary of the prophet Jeremiah and approximately the same age as Ezekiel, who mentions him in his prophecy (Ezekiel 14:14, 20; 28:3).

ATTACKS ON THE BOOK OF DANIEL

Daniel is one of the books most often attacked by destructive critics of the Bible. We can be glad that the Lord Jesus Christ has pronounced the book genuine and authentic. (Note the reference above to Matthew 24:15.) The attacks of those who do not accept the book of Daniel as genuine have been largely in four areas: *miracles, predictions, language,* and *history.*

If the book of Daniel were to be rejected simply because it contains *miracles,* then hardly any portion of the Scriptures could be accepted. To one who does not know God, miracles seem impossible. The miraculous is believable, however, to one who knows Him who created all things. Furthermore, as in other parts of Scripture, the miracles in Daniel are related with soberness and restraint, without the fantastic elements connected with myths and legends of false religions.

The detailed *predictions* in Daniel, many of which were fulfilled in the period between Daniel and the coming of Christ, have caused some unbelievers to reject the book. They assert that the accurate and detailed picture of the persecution of the Jews by Antiochus Epiphanes in the second century before Christ could not possibly have been written four centuries before that time, but must have been written after the events had actually taken place. Such a denial of the supernatural element in prophecy overlooks the ancient testimony to the book of Daniel, notably the references to Daniel himself in the book of Ezekiel, already referred to; allusions to Daniel in the Apocryphal Books, which were written in the period between the Old and the New Testaments; and allusions to Daniel in the writings of Josephus, the Jewish historian of the first century of the Christian Era. Besides, other parts of Scripture contain equally detailed descriptions which were exactly fulfilled.

The book of Daniel has been attacked because it contains *some Persian words* and *three Greek words,* the names of musical instruments. (See chapter 3.) But Daniel lived on into the Persian period. Therefore, it is not at all surprising that some Persian words should occur in the book. Moreover, modern research has shown the antiquity of Greek civilization and the widespread nature of Greek commerce earlier than the time of Daniel. It has even been discovered that Nebuchadnezzar of Babylon employed Greek mercenary troops. It is not unlikely that these soldiers brought along some of their native musical instruments and, with the instruments, their accustomed names.

The attack from *history* has centered largely around the mention, in the book, of Belshazzar. This argument has long ago become outmoded, however, since cuneiform inscriptions have been unearthed mentioning Belshazzar.

All these attacks have as their object the discrediting of

the book of Daniel as a reliable historical record. Most of the destructive critics regard it as a work of historical fiction, produced in the second century B.C. However, these negative attacks sink into insignificance when weighed against the positive testimony for the genuineness of the book. To reject the book of Daniel, is to discount the witness of the Lord Jesus Christ Himself. This should be the deciding factor for the Christian.

THE HISTORICAL BACKGROUND OF DANIEL

The historical background of the book of Daniel is found in the closing chapters of II Kings and II Chronicles, as well as in portions of the book of Jeremiah.

Daniel was taken to Babylon at the time of the first Babylonian invasion of Judah, as already mentioned (606 B.C.). At that time, comparatively few of the people of Judah were carried away to Babylon. Those who were taken captive seem to have been mostly youths from the noble classes. A second deportation took place late in 598 or early in 597, when King Jehoiachin and many others were transported to the enemy land. The third and final stage of the Babylonian captivity came with the capture and destruction of the city of Jerusalem in the eleventh year of the reign of Zedekiah, 586 B.C. It can be seen, then, that Daniel had been in Babylon for twenty years at the time Jerusalem was destroyed. During that twenty-year period, the great prophet Jeremiah was engaged in the latter half of his long ministry in Jerusalem. As we have seen, another contemporary, the prophet Ezekiel, who was taken to Babylon along with King Jehoiachin, began to prophesy about 593 and continued for more than twenty years (Ezekiel 1:1-3).

THE STRUCTURE OF DANIEL

In its structure the book of Daniel is quite simple. Some would divide it according to the languages in which it was written. This is not apparent, of course, in the English translation. From the beginning of the book through 2:3, the Hebrew language is used. The portion from 2:4 through the end of chapter 7 is in Aramaic, a language closely related to Hebrew and used in Babylon in Daniel's time. From 8:1 to the end of the book, Hebrew is used again.

The easiest division for the average reader of the English Bible is that which views the book in two parts, according to its contents. It is evident that the last six chapters are different from the first six. In the first six chapters, there are important revelations of the future, but the framework is historical. We read of the personal history of Daniel in Babylon during the time of the Babylonian and Medo-Persian empires. The second half of the book contains the visions of Daniel, some of which supplement and amplify the information given in the first half. Here the framework itself is prophetic.

Consequently, the basic outline can be remembered without difficulty:

I. THE HISTORY OF DANIEL IN BABYLON (chapters 1—6)

II. THE VISIONS OF DANIEL (chapters 7—12)

Another factor that makes the contents of Daniel easy to remember is that in the first division each chapter contains a complete story in itself. One should not have any trouble thinking through these chapters. The second division consists of four separate visions given to Daniel. Consequently, we can fill in the outline as follows:

1. **The History of Daniel in Babylon (chapters 1—6)**
    a. Daniel's Early Adventures in Babylon (1)
    b. Nebuchadnezzar's Dream of the Image (2)
    c. Daniel's Friends in the Fiery Furnace (3)
    d. The Humbling of Nebuchadnezzar (4)
    e. Belshazzar and the Handwriting on the Wall (5)
    f. Daniel in the Den of Lions (6)

2. **The Visions of Daniel (chapters 7—12)**
    a. The Vision of the Four Beasts (7)
    b. The Vision of the Ram and the He-goat (8)
    c. Daniel's Prayer and the Vision of the Seventy Weeks (9)

d. The Vision of the Glory of God and the Prophetic Future (10—12)

A FEW HIGH LIGHTS OF THE BOOK

Daniel—"a Man Greatly Beloved"

The first chapter of Daniel is the necessary introduction to the rest of the book. In it we see how Daniel came to be in Babylon, and how he gained a place of prominence and favor. Daniel was a youth with real purpose. We do not know his age at the time he was taken to Babylon, but he could scarcely be past his late teens at the outset of the three-year training period (1:5). Undoubtedly, Daniel based his steadfast purpose squarely upon the Word of God. To partake of the king's food would bring him into disobedience to the law which God had given. (See, for example, Leviticus 11.) Daniel is seen throughout his life as an exemplary character. God calls him "a man greatly beloved" (10:11).

Four Great World Empires

In Nebuchadnezzar's dream (chapter 2), and in the vision of the four beasts (chapter 7), four great world empires are described which would control the history of the people of Israel during the long period called by the Lord Jesus "the times of the Gentiles" (Luke 21:24). These four empires are the Babylonian; the Medo-Persian; the Greek, or Macedonian; and the Roman. (See the accompanying chart.)

The Seventy Sevens of Years

It seems evident, from chapter 9 especially, that the present age is not directly in view in the book of Daniel, and that the Roman Empire, which was in control at the time of the first coming of the Lord Jesus, will be restored and will again be in control in a different form just prior to the second coming of Christ. The seventy "weeks" (literally, "seventy sevens") described in chap-

World Empires	Nebuchadnezzar's Dream	Daniel's Dreams	
	Daniel 2:31-45	Daniel 7:1-28	Daniel 8:1-27
Babylonian	Head of gold	Lion	
Medo-Persian	Breast and arms of silver	Bear	Ram
Grecian	Belly and thighs of brass	Leopard	He-goat
Roman	Legs of iron	The beast with ten horns	
Antichrist's	Ten toes of iron and clay		
Christ's	The stone cut out without hands		

ter 9 cover the history of the nation of Israel and the city of Jerusalem. Sixty-nine of these seven-year periods (or 483 years) elapsed between the time of the decree for the building of the city and the ministry of the Lord Jesus Christ. The crucifixion of Christ alluded to in 9:26 occurred after the close of the sixty-ninth week, but before the opening of the seventieth week. The whole present age forms a great gap, or parenthesis, during which Israel's times and seasons are not being reckoned. The seventieth week of years will not begin until a future prince or ruler (9:26) makes a covenant with the Jewish people. This seven-year period is often spoken of as the tribulation period. After three and a half years, this ruler, often called Antichrist, will break the covenant and begin a terrible persecution of the Jewish people. The second half of the seventieth week is the period known in Scripture as "the great tribulation."

The Pivotal Nature of the Book Illustrated

While it is impossible in this brief, elementary survey

to study the details of the book of Daniel, the mention of these things is sufficient to show the pivotal nature of the book in the prophetic Scriptures generally.

Personal Application of These Truths

Along with the knowledge of prophecy, so necessary if we are to understand God's purpose, should come the personal application of these truths to our own lives, in order that we may come closer to the Lord Jesus and live lives of purity, in constant expectation of His return. *10*

Survey of the Scriptures
A Moody Correspondence Course

Exam 10
Lessons 19, 20

Name_____ (Print plainly)   Exam Grade_____

Address_____ Date_____

City_____ State_____ Zip Code_____   Class Number_____

Instructor_____

LESSON 19   EZEKIEL

In the blank space at the right-hand margin write "True" or "False" after each of the following statements:

1. Ezekiel and King Zedekiah were taken into captivity at the same time. _____

2. An apocalyptic prophecy is one which is given through pictorial vision. _____

3. Ezekiel's prophecy against Tyre contained an allusion to Satan. _____

4. Gog and Magog will invade Israel from the south in the end time. _____

5. God promised Ezekiel that the people to whom he prophesied would heed His Word. _____

255

In the blank space write the letter of the correct or most nearly correct answer.

6. Ezekiel was a

   a. prophet and a priest.
   b. priest and a king.
   c. king and a prophet.
   d. prophet only. _____

7. The three men who by their righteousness could not have saved Jerusalem were

   a. Noah, Abraham, and David.
   b. Daniel, David, and Job.
   c. Abraham, Isaac, and Jacob.
   d. Daniel, Job, and Noah. _____

8. Ezekiel's vision of the valley of dry bones pictures

   a. the resurrection of Christ.
   b. the restoration of life to the nation of Israel.
   c. the resurrection of the wicked dead.
   d. the revival of the Roman Empire. _____

9. Name the king, prophets or event indicated on this chart by the following letters:

   a. _____

   b. _____

   c. _____

   d. _____

Judah	Prophets	World Powers
	626 B.C.	
A		• Babylon overthrows Assyria
Jehoahaz		
Jehoiakim	B	• 1st Babylonian invasion of Judah
Jehoiachin	593 B.C.	• 2nd Babylonian invasion of Judah
Zedekiah		
		• 3rd Babylonian invasion of Judah
Babylonian captivity	? C	• Jerusalem taken and temple destroyed Babylonian captivity begins 586 B.C. • D
	571 B.C.	
		• Medo-Persia overthrows Babylon

Use Your Bible

You may use your Bible to complete the remainder of this exam.

10. Read the following Scripture passages and check (√) in the appropriate blank spaces the prophet or prophets who included in their prophecies the Gentile nations listed below.

    Isaiah 13:1; 15:1; 17:1; 18:1; 19:1; 21:11, 13; 23:1
    Jeremiah 46:2; 47:1; 48:1; 49:1, 7, 23, 34; 50:1
    Ezekiel 25:2, 8, 12, 15; 26:2; 29:2, 19; 30:4; 32:22, 24, 30

	Isaiah	Jeremiah	Ezekiel
Ammonites			
Arabia			
Asshur (Assyria)			
Babylon			
Damascus			
Edom (Dumah)			
Elam			
Egypt			
Ethiopia			
Moab			
Philistines			
Tyre (Tyrus)			
Zidonians (Sidonians)			

LESSON 20   DANIEL

In the blank space at the right-hand margin write "True" or "False" after each of the following statements:

11. Daniel is written both in Hebrew and in Arabic. _____

12. The history of Israel, prophetically, was revealed to Daniel in his vision of the seventy "**weeks.**" _____

13. The second half of the seventieth week is known as the Millennium. _____

14. The life of purity Daniel lived in Babylon challenges us to live pure lives also. _____

15. Name the kings, prophets or event indicated on this chart by the following letters:

    a. _____

    b. _____

    c. _____

    d. _____

    e. _____

    _____

Judah	Prophets	World Powers
Josiah	626 B.C.	
		• Babylon overthrows Assyria
Jehoahaz		
Jehoiakim	JEREMIAH 606 B.C.	• E
A	593 B.C.	• 2nd Babylonian invasion of Judah
B		
Babylonian captivity	? C	• 3rd Babylonian invasion of Judah • Jerusalem taken and temple destroyed Babylonian captivity begins 586 B.C. • Babylon overthrows Egypt
	D	
	571 B.C.	
		• Medo-Persia overthrows Babylon

16. Name the items indicated on the chart below by the following letters:

    a. _____

    b. _____

    c. _____

    d. _____

    e. _____

    f. _____

World Empires	Nebuchadnezzar's Dream Daniel 2:31-45	Daniel's Dreams	
		Daniel 7:1-28	Daniel 8:1-27
Babylonian	Head of gold	B	
Medo-Persian	Breast and arms of silver	C	E
Grecian	Belly and thighs of brass	D	F
Roman	Legs of iron	The beast with ten horns	
Antichrist's	Ten toes of iron and clay		
Christ's	A		

258

17. *Complete the following outline of the book of Daniel:*

	Chapters
I. The History of Daniel in Babylon	1—6
1. Daniel's Early Adventures in Babylon	1
2. _____	2
3. Daniel's Friends in the Fiery Furnace	3
4. The Humbling of Nebuchadnezzar	4
5. _____	5
6. Daniel in the Den of Lions	6
II. The Visions of Daniel	7—12
1. The Vision of the Four Beasts	7
2. _____	8
3. _____	9
4. _____	10—12

Reading Chart

Check (×) the chapters you have read.

EZEKIEL					5				10
			15			20			25
			30			35			40
			45						
DANIEL						5			10

_____MAIL TO ADDRESS ON BACK COVER.

Lesson 21

Hosea—Joel—Amos

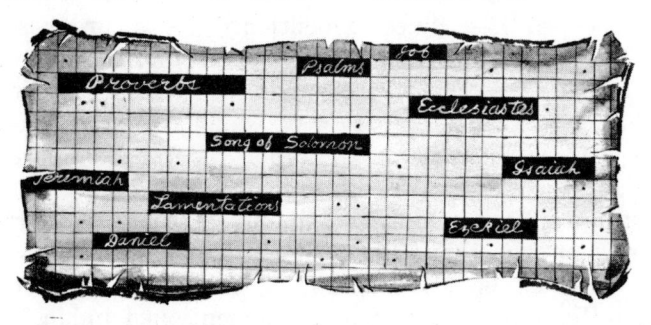

(Illustration of a scroll/chart listing: Proverbs, Psalms, Job, Ecclesiastes, Song of Solomon, Isaiah, Jeremiah, Lamentations, Daniel, Ezekiel)

Judah	Prophets	Israel	World Powers
Athaliah			
Joash	? 825 B.C. **JOEL** ?	Jehu	• Syria strong
		Jehoahaz	
		Jehoash	
Amaziah		Jeroboam II	• Jonah preached to Nineveh about this time?
	AMOS ?		
Uzziah		Zachariah	
		Shallum	
		Menahem	
	740 B.C. **HOSEA**	Pekahiah	
Jotham		Pekah	• 2½ tribes east of Jordan taken captive by Assyria
Ahaz	**ISAIAH**	Hoshea	
Hezekiah		Assyrian captivity	• Fall of Samaria 722 B.C. Assyrian captivity begins
II Kings 12—20	*Hosea 1:1* ?	*II Kings 3—17*	

The twelve books from Hosea through Malachi are often referred to as the Minor Prophets. This title, however, does not mean that these books are unimportant. It refers, rather, to their length. They are all very brief as compared with the books of Isaiah, Jeremiah, and Ezekiel.

HOSEA

The prophet of God who wrote this book is called Hosea, the son of Beeri (1:1). In the Authorized Version of Romans 9:25 he is called Osee. Since he mentioned that he prophesied during the reigns of Uzziah, Jotham, Ahaz, and Hezekiah in Judah, and in the days of Jeroboam II in Israel (1:1), it is clear that he was a contemporary of Isaiah (compare Isaiah 1:1), and that Amos was a somewhat older contemporary (Amos 1:1).

Hosea's prophecy is addressed mainly to Israel, the northern kingdom, but there are also numerous references to Judah. Just as Isaiah prophesying to Judah mentioned Israel, so Hosea prophesying to Israel mentioned Judah. The book shows the intimate relationship between the two kingdoms and recognizes the house of David as the rightful rulers (1:1; 3:5; 8:4).

From the dating in the book itself we can conclude that Hosea's ministry took place in the third quarter of the eighth century B.C. (about 750 to 725). He was one of the last of God's messengers to the Kingdom of Israel before its overthrow by the Assyrians (Samaria fell 722 B.C.). Israel, because of its sin, is seen as soon to be taken captive. The tragic experience within the prophet's own family served as a fitting object lesson for the sinful nation.

The theme of Hosea may be stated thus: Israel, the unfaithful wife of the LORD. The love and tenderness of the prophet for his unfaithful wife furnish an illustration of the persistent and consistent love of God toward the nation which He had chosen and which has been so unfaithful to Him. As in some of the other prophets, idolatry is identified as spiritual adultery. The fervent plea of God toward this faithless nation is expressed repeatedly by the word *return* (note especially in this connection 14:1).

The structure of the book may be shown as follows:

I. THE PROPHET'S EXPERIENCE (chapters 1—3)

II. THE PROPHET'S TEACHING (chapters 4—14)

Both by object lesson and by direct statement, God reminds the nation (often called Ephraim from the leading tribe) of its sinfulness in departing from Him, and of His continuing love. Some critics of the Bible have mistakenly supposed that the love of God is seen only in the New Testament. It could scarcely be expressed any more plainly or poignantly than in this Old Testament prophet. As Hosea purchased Gomer from the slave market, where she had gone after a period of shame and degradation, so God will yet restore disloyal Israel. The prophecy looks far into the future to the kingdom of Christ. Israel is now in the "many days" described in 3:4, but the time foretold in 3:5 will yet come.

Hosea tells plainly of many sins of the nation. The style of his prophecy is somewhat abrupt and abounding in figures of speech. Its staccato tone vividly portrays the heart agony of God over the sinning nation which He loved. "O Israel, thou hast destroyed thyself; but in me is thine help. I will be thy king: where is any other that may save thee in all thy cities?" (13:9, 10).

There are a number of quotations from Hosea in the New Testament. One of the most striking is 6:6, quoted twice by the Lord Jesus to show the need for reality in religious worship (Matthew 9:13; 12:7).

After the necessary judgment from God because of sin, there is a blessed restoration: "I will heal their backsliding, I will love them freely: for mine anger is turned away from him" (14:4). As in so many of the prophets, the glorious future of Israel is presented, a future which is bound up with the Messiah, the Lord Jesus Christ.

JOEL

This book, unlike many of the prophets, bears no date. Its writer, Joel, says nothing directly concerning himself except that he was the son of Pethuel. It seems clear from the book itself that the prophet lived in Judah and ministered to that nation (compare 1:9, 13, 14; 2:9, 15-17; 3:3, 4-6).

The position of this book in the Hebrew Bible shows that it was regarded by ancient Hebrew scholars as being among the earliest of the writing prophets. It bears similarity to Amos (compare Joel 3:16 with Amos 1:2; Joel 3:18 with

Amos 9:13). The mention of priests and elders without any mention of a king has caused some scholars to place it in the time of the boyhood of Joash, when Jehoiada the priest was influential. It is likely that Joel lived late in the ninth century B.C., perhaps around 825.

The book of Joel tells of a great plague of insects which came upon the land of Judah as a judgment from God against sin. In the law, God had promised material prosperity to His people for obedience, and adversity for disobedience. The period described in the opening prophecy was one of famine and suffering because an enormous hoard of insects had eaten much of the vegetation. The distress in Judah because of this judgment is seen as a foreshadowing of greater distress in a coming day of greater judgment. That yet future period is described as "the day of Jehovah" (A.S.V.; "the day of the LORD," A.V.). This phrase may be considered as the theme of the book. "The day of Jehovah" is the time of God's judgment upon the earth in connection with the second coming of Christ.

A simple, basic outline of the book is as follows:

I. THE PLAGUE OF INSECTS AND "THE DAY OF THE LORD" (chapters 1:1—2:27)

II. BLESSING AND JUDGMENT IN THE LAST DAYS (chapters 2:28—3:21)

The great prophecy of the outpouring of the Holy Spirit (2:28-32) was quoted by Peter in his sermon on the Day of Pentecost (Acts 2:16-21). Peter does not state that everything prophesied in the passage in Joel was fulfilled that day, but he indicates that the Day of Pentecost was the beginning of the period called "the last days." The wonders in the heaven and in the earth are to precede "the great and the terrible day of the LORD" (Joel 2:31; Acts 2:20). In the meantime, salvation is offered to all of those who call on His name.

AMOS

The prophet Amos, as we have seen, was an older contemporary of Hosea. His home was in Tekoa, a town in the Kingdom of Judah, about ten miles south of Jerusalem. His ministry, however, was to the Kingdom of Israel, specifically at Bethel, the site of an idolatrous shrine (7:13). Nevertheless, Amos had a message for the "whole family" (3:1), the "house of Jacob" (3:13).

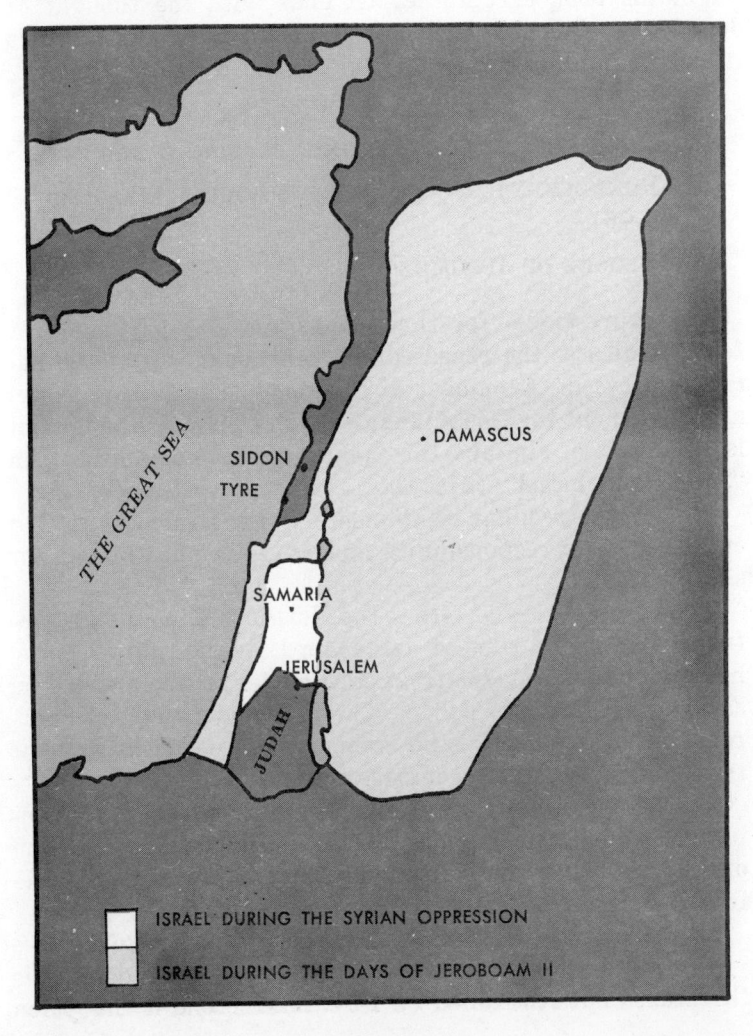

ISRAEL DURING THE SYRIAN OPPRESSION

ISRAEL DURING THE DAYS OF JEROBOAM II

In the time of Jeroboam II, the Kingdom of Israel was outwardly prosperous and enlarged (compare II Kings 14: 23-29). Yet in spite of external prosperity, Israel was corrupt and deserved the impending judgment of God. Amos, who identifies himself as a herdman and a gatherer of sycamore fruit (7:12-14), informs us that he had no prophetic background but that God had called him specifically to go and prophesy to Israel, and to announce judgment. Every chapter of his book except the last ends with the thought of doom. He rebukes Israel for sin and injustice and reminds it of accountability to God.

The structure of the book is threefold:

I. JUDGMENT ON THE NATIONS (chapters 1 and 2)

II. PUNISHMENT OF ISRAEL FOR INIQUITY (chapters 3—6)

III. VISIONS OF JUDGMENT (chapters 7—9)

The expression, "for three transgressions . . . and for four," indicates the repeated and continuous sin of the nation addressed. A number of kingdoms surrounding Israel are singled out for God's judgment. In every case judgment is the result of sin, and this judgment will come also upon "Judah and Israel" (2:4, 6).

In fact, the peculiar relationship which Israel has to God entails greater responsibility and requires punishment for sin (3:2).

The very religion of Israel, the Northern Kingdom, is sinful; for from the time of Jeroboam I, every king of Israel had maintained the idolatrous sanctuaries at Dan and Bethel as a settled national policy. The repeated ritual is abhorrent to God, for there is no accompanying heart attitude of trust and submission (compare 5:21-27).

The luxury that was prevalent in the prophet's day (compare 6:4) was accompanied by social injustices, oppression of the poor, widespread drunkenness and immorality. Therefore, judgment had to fall.

In the closing division of the book, Amos is given five visions. The first is that of the locusts, in which judgment is threatened but restrained (7:1-3). The second is the vision of the fire, in which the same thought is repeated (7:4-6). This is followed by the vision of the plumbline, in which it is seen that judgment is determined (7:7-9). Following the interlude which tells of the prophet's experience at Bethel (7:10-17), the fourth vision, that of the basket of summer fruit (chapter 8), indicates that judgment is near. Finally, the vision of "the Lord standing upon the altar" (9:1-10) looks toward the actual execution of the judgment.

Here, as always in the prophets, certain judgment is followed by certain restoration and blessing in the kingdom age. This is described in the closing paragraph of the prophecy (9:11-15), a portion of which is quoted by James at the council in Jerusalem (Acts 15:15-17).

Self Check Test 11

What have you learned about Hosea, Joel and Amos?

In the right-hand column circle the following statements "true" or "false":

1. The minor prophets are less important than the major prophets. (p. 261)   T   F

2. Hosea prophesied mainly to Israel but also referred to Judah. (p. 262)   T   F

3. In Hosea idolatry is identified as spiritual adultery. (p. 262)   T   F

4. Amos came from a family which had given many prophets to Israel. (p. 266)

5. Joel was regarded by ancient Hebrew scholars as one of the earliest of the writing prophets. (p. 263)   T   F

6. Hosea was a contemporary of Zechariah and Malachi. (p. 262)   T   F

7. Amos came from the country to prophesy to Israel concerning union with Judah. (p. 266)   T   F

8. Joel is thought to have lived and prophesied in Israel. (p. 263)   T   F

9. Hosea's prophecy was based on his own domestic bliss. (p. 262)   T   F

10. Peter declared on the Day of Pentecost that everything Joel predicted was being fulfilled then. (p. 264)   T   F

11. *Complete the following outlines:*

HOSEA	Chapters
I. _____	1—3
II. _____ (p. 262)	4—14
JOEL	
I. _____	1:1—2:27
II. _____ (p. 264)	2:28—3:21
AMOS	
I. _____	1 and 2
II. _____	3—6
III. _____ (p. 266)	7—9

Dig Deeper in Your Bible

12. The following groups of verses describe the characteristics listed below which were true of the national life in Israel during the days of Hosea and Amos. Write the correct letter in each blank space.

   a. Amos 2:6; 5:11
   b. Hosea 2:13; 4:12, 17; Amos 5:21-26
   c. Hosea 2:8; 12:8; 13:6; Amos 3:15; 6:4-8
   d. Hosea 4:1, 2
   e. Amos 6:13 ("Horns are the Hebrew symbol of military power.")

   The material prosperity of Israel   _____

   The military attitude of Israel   _____

   The religious apostasy of Israel   _____

   The social inequality in Israel   _____

   The moral depravity of Israel   _____

Turn to page 309 to find the correct answers.
Please do not send the answers to the Correspondence School.

Lesson 22

Obadiah—Jonah—Micah

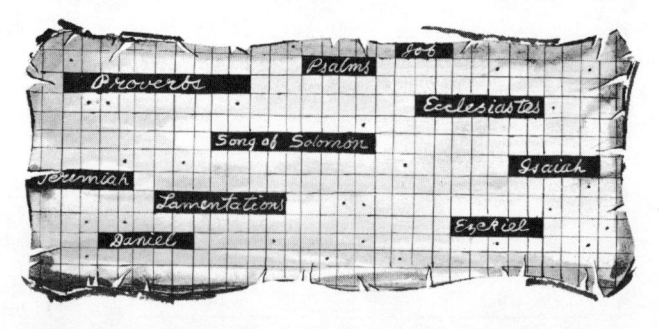

Judah	Prophets	Israel	World Powers
Jehoram 848-841 B.C.	? OBADIAH ?	Jehoram	• Revolt of Edom against Judah
Ahaziah			
Athaliah		Jehu	
Joash		Jehoahaz	
		Jehoash	
Amaziah	? JONAH ?	Jeroboam II 782-753 B.C.	
Uzziah		Zachariah	
		Shallum	
		Menahem	
	?	Pekahiah	• 2½ tribes east of Jordan taken captive by Assyria
Jotham		Pekah	
Ahaz	MICAH ISAIAH	Hoshea	• Fall of Samaria 722 B.C. Assyrian captivity begins
Hezekiah	?	Assyrian captivity	• Assyrians invade Judah God intervenes to save Jerusalem
II Kings 8—20	Micah 1:1	II Kings 14:25 II Kings 3—17 II Kings 8:16-20	

OBADIAH

Obadiah is the shortest book in the Old Testament. Of all the books of the prophets, this is the most difficult to place chronologically. Even conservative Bible scholars have dis-

270

agreed widely, some placing Obadiah as the earliest of the writing prophets and others dating the book after the destruction of Jerusalem by the Babylonians in 586 B.C. This is not an essential matter. The substance of the book is unchanged, no matter what date is assigned to it. In the opinion of the present writer, however, an early date is preferable. This seems to be indicated by the position of the book in the Hebrew canon, between Amos and Jonah. While these books of the Minor Prophets are not in chronological order, it is apparent that the ancient Hebrew scholars who arranged them attempted to put the earlier books at the head of the list. Those who take the late date argue that there was no such despoiling of Jerusalem as is mentioned in the book earlier than the time of the Babylonian captivity. It is possible, though, that this may be a reference to the troubles in the time of King Jehoram, who reigned from about 848 to 841 B.C. (described in II Chronicles 21:8-17).

The theme of Obadiah is *God's judgment upon Edom,* the nation descended from Esau, the brother of Jacob (compare Genesis 36).

This prophecy of judgment is not the expression of personal hatred or bigotry on the part of the prophet Obadiah. It is, rather, the solemn judgment of God upon the sinful nation. Other prophets wrote various prophecies concerning a number of nations surrounding Israel. Obadiah's theme is limited to this one nation, which had done so much harm to the people of God.

In the first nine verses, the doom of Edom is announced. Because the Edomite cities were built in rocky cliffs, the inhabitants considered themselves safe and their fortresses impregnable. God tells them that this is a false security, and that He will bring them down. Three things that will not save them are their rocky fortresses (verses 3 and 4), their allies (verse 7), and their own wise and mighty men (verses 8 and 9).

The second paragraph (verses 10-16) tells the reason for God's judgment upon Edom. Their violence against Israel and the aid which they have given to those who despoiled Jerusalem are cited as a cause of doom. The judgment which is coming upon Edom is in connection with "the day of the LORD." There is evidently here a nearer view and a far view, for Edom's literal destruction came soon after the destruction of Judah when the Babylonians conquered that nation. But that visitation of God's judgment foreshadows the future day of the LORD, His judgment upon the earth. This is the time of retribution: "As thou hast done, it shall be done unto thee: thy reward shall return upon thine own head" (verse 15).

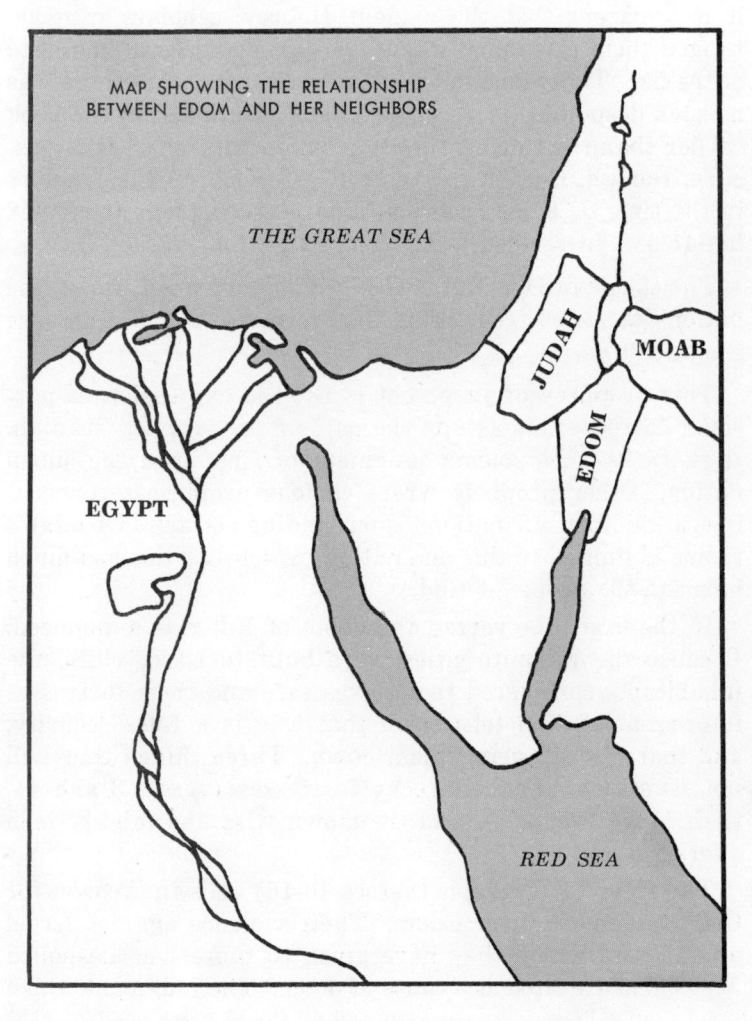

MAP SHOWING THE RELATIONSHIP BETWEEN EDOM AND HER NEIGHBORS

THE GREAT SEA

EGYPT

JUDAH

MOAB

EDOM

RED SEA

In the final paragraph of the prophecy (verses 17-21) God promises future deliverance for His people and announces that "the house of Jacob shall possess their possessions" (verse 17). The triumphant proclamation at the close of the prophecy awaits fulfillment at the second coming of Christ: "And the kingdom shall be the LORD'S" (verse 21).

Therefore, the book of Obadiah may be outlined as follows:

    I. THE DOOM OF EDOM (verses 1-9)

    II. THE REASON FOR GOD'S JUDGMENT UPON EDOM (verses 10-16)

    III. GOD'S PROMISE OF FUTURE DELIVERANCE FOR ISRAEL (verses 17-21)

JONAH

The book of Jonah has been much attacked and ridiculed by destructive critics of the Bible. It is different from the other books of the prophets in that it relates an experience of the prophet himself rather than the message which God gave him to announce. The Lord Jesus Christ fully authenticated the book of Jonah (see especially Matthew 12:40). The use which the Lord Jesus made of Jonah's experience shows that He accepted it as actual history. To deny the historicity of the book is to disagree with the Lord of glory.

The writer calls himself Jonah the son of Amittai (1:1). Since he is mentioned in II Kings 14:25 as the herald of a prophecy which was fulfilled in the days of Jeroboam II of Israel, it is evident that he lived either before Jeroboam's reign or at least early in that reign. It is generally believed that Jonah lived about the year 800 B.C. God's mission to Jonah was to prophesy to and against Nineveh, the capital of the Assyrian Empire, located on the Tigris River. In response to Jonah's preaching, the people of Nineveh repented and were granted a respite by God. The later prophecy of Nahum, however, shows that this repentance was only temporary, and that God eventually had to bring destruction upon this wicked city and empire.

The chapter divisions of Jonah form a convenient outline of the book:

I. JONAH'S FIRST COMMISSION FROM THE LORD AND HIS DISOBEDIENCE (chapter 1)

II. JONAH'S PRAYER AND DELIVERANCE (chapter 2)

III. JONAH'S SECOND COMMISSION AND OBEDIENCE (chapter 3)

IV. GOD'S OBJECT LESSON IN COMPASSION AND MERCY (chapter 4)

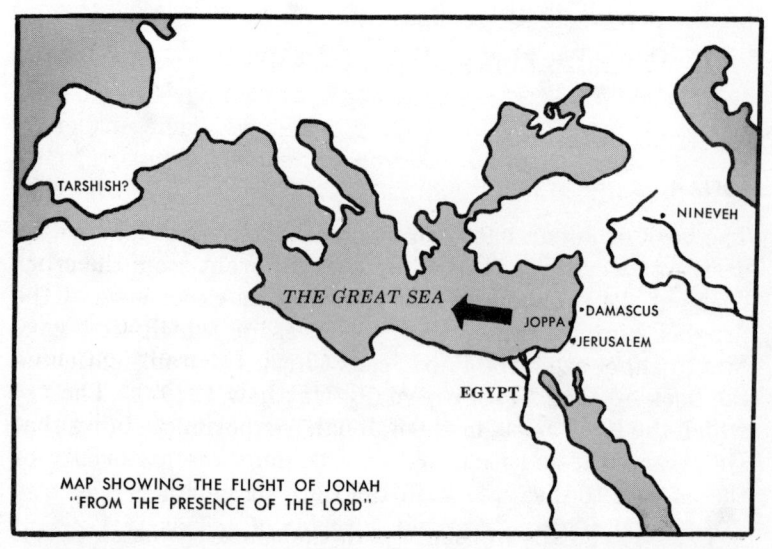

MAP SHOWING THE FLIGHT OF JONAH "FROM THE PRESENCE OF THE LORD"

Because Jonah did not wish to go to Nineveh to fulfill the will of God, he attempted to go as far as possible in the other direction. It is thought that Tarshish (verse 3) is a region on the coast of Spain. Although Jonah probably was familiar with Psalm 139, in his self-centered folly he seemed to think that he could get away from God. The great sea creature which God prepared was in a sense an instrument of judgment, but in another sense an instrument of deliverance for the rebellious prophet. One should note that this was a *prepared* creature. The word used in the Hebrew, as well as the Greek word used in the quotation in Matthew 12:40, does not specifically state whether this creature was a fish or a mammal. Certainly one who knows God cannot doubt His power to prepare a creature capable of swallowing a man.

Jonah's prayer in chapter 2 is in the form of a psalm. Possibly no one has prayed under stranger circumstances. The prophet recognizes that he is figuratively dead, that there is no deliverance apart from the mercy of God. As he feels the great creature descending to the sea floor (2:6), as he becomes entangled in the vegetation which it has swallowed (verse 5), he is fully aware of the hopelessness of his plight. Then acknowledging that God can deliver, he promises to fulfill his vow (verse 9). God then restores him to land and recommissions him.

An even greater miracle than that of the great fish is the repentance of Nineveh at Jonah's preaching, for this involves the hearts of men. The Lord Jesus, commenting on this in connection with the unbelief in His own day, said, "The men of Nineveh shall rise in judgment with this generation, and shall condemn it: because they repented at the preaching of Jonas; and, behold, a greater than Jonas is here" (Matthew 12:41).

God's sparing the Ninevites when they repented, caused Jonah to be angry. No doubt, as an intensely patriotic Israelite, he recognized the terrible threat which Assyria was to his own nation. Consequently, he wanted to see the Assyrians destroyed.

God teaches him a lesson through three other *prepared* things. (Note four prepared things in this book, 1:17; 4:6; 4:7; 4:8.) The lesson is this: Jonah can be greatly concerned about so trivial a thing as a gourd vine, which has been a benefit to him, but remain utterly unconcerned about the fate of thousands of people. God shows the unreasonable prophet His mercy and compassion.

MICAH

The prophet Micah was a younger contemporary of Isaiah. (Compare Micah 1:1 with Isaiah 1:1.) He was from the town of Moresheth-gath, southwest of Jerusalem; but his prophecy is addressed to both kingdoms, Israel and Judah

(1:1). One of the best-known prophecies in the Old Testament is found in Micah 5:2, the prediction of the birthplace of the coming Saviour. This is referred to in Matthew 2:6. More than seven hundred years before Christ was born, God said He would be born in Bethlehem of Judah.

There are three messages in the prophecy of Micah, each one introduced by the word "Hear" (1:2; 3:1; 6:1).

The first message, addressed to all the people (1:2), describes *God's witness against Israel*. Judgment is coming because of sin. Samaria, the capital of the Northern Kingdom, is to be destroyed (1:6). The second message, addressed to the leaders of the people, shows *the failure of princes* (3:1), *prophets* (3:5), *and priests* (3:11). Zion, or Jerusalem, is to suffer the same fate as Samaria (3:12). To these false and sinful leaders God proclaims the coming of *His Ruler in Israel* (5:2), even the Messiah, the Lord Jesus Christ. This section contains a number of references to the distant future as well as to the prophet's own day. The description of the coming millennial Kingdom in chapter 4 is parallel to the similar prophecy in Isaiah 2.

The closing message, again addressed to all the people, is called in the text "the LORD'S controversy" (6:2). Mingled with the note of judgment, certain to come, is the companion note, so often seen in the prophets, of future restoration and blessing. As Dr. James M. Gray says: "The end of this book is peculiarly affecting, presenting a kind of soliloquy of repentance on Israel's part. The better element, the right-spirited ones, are confessing and lamenting their sinful condition, but expressing confidence in God's returning favor. There are few passages in the Bible more expressive of profound and quiet hope and trust than this one" (7:7-20).

The rhetorical question of verse 18, "Who is a God like unto thee. . . ?" has been used as the refrain of one of the great hymns, *Great God of Wonders*. God is indeed the One who pardons transgressions through His Son, who was born in Bethlehem, and who will yet be Ruler in Israel.

Survey of the Scriptures
A Moody Correspondence Course

Exam 11
Lessons 21, 22

Name_____ Exam Grade_____
(Print plainly)

Address_____ Date_____

City_____State_____Zip Code_____ Class Number_____

Instructor_____

LESSON 21   HOSEA—JOEL—AMOS

In the blank space at the right-hand margin write "True" or "False" after each of the following statements:

1. Every chapter in Amos, except the last, ends with the thought of doom. _____

2. Hosea's prophecy looks forward to the future kingdom of Christ. _____

3. Hosea is never quoted in the New Testament. _____

4. Joel bases his prophecy of judgment on a then recent plague of insects which had devastated the land. _____

5. Everything Joel had to say about the outpouring of the Holy Spirit was fulfilled on the Day of Pentecost. _____

In the blank space write the letter of the correct or most nearly correct answer.

6. Hosea was a contemporary of
    a. Isaiah and Amos.
    b. Jeremiah and Ezekiel.
    c. Zechariah and Malachi.
    d. Daniel and Haggai.   _____

7. Hosea's prophecy was based on
    a. his domestic happiness.
    b. the tragedy of his wife's unfaithfulness.
    c. his experiences as an unmarried man.
    d. the wickedness of his children.   _____

8. Joel is thought to have lived
    a. in Israel and prophesied to Judah.
    b. in Judah and prophesied to Israel.
    c. in and prophesied to Israel.
    d. in and prophesied to Judah.   _____

9. Amos came from the country to prophesy to Israel concerning
    a. blessing.
    b. judgment.
    c. revival.
    d. union with Judah.   _____

10. Name the prophet, the king or the event indicated on this chart by the following letters:

Judah	Prophets	Israel	World Powers
Athaliah			
Joash	? 825 B.C. [A] ?	Jehu	• Syria strong
		Jehoahaz	
Amaziah		Jehoash	• E
		D	
Uzziah	? [B]	Zachariah / Shallum	
		Menahem	
	740 B.C. [C]	Pekahiah	
Jotham		Pekah	• 2½ tribes east of Jordan taken captive by Assyria
Ahaz	ISAIAH	Hoshea	• Fall of Samaria 722 B.C. Assyrian captivity begins
Hezekiah	?	Assyrian captivity	

a. _____

b. _____

c. _____

d. _____

e. _____

11. Name four of the five visions given to Amos.

a. _____

b. _____

c. _____

d. _____

Use Your Bible

You may use your Bible to answer the next question.

12. Both Amos and Hosea began to foretell the downfall of Israel during the days of Jeroboam II. This king of Israel recovered all the territory which, in the most prosperous times of the united kingdom, had been conquered by David or occupied by Solomon. (See map on page 265.) The questions which follow are designed to help you picture the characteristics of national life in Israel which called forth the terrible warnings of these two prophets.

After reading the following Scripture portions describe briefly (but specifically) the characteristics of Israel's national life.

a. The material prosperity of Israel
   Hosea 2:8; 12:8; 13:6; Amos 3:15; 6:4-8

   _____

   _____

   _____

b. The military attitude of Israel
   Amos 6:13

   _____

c. The religious apostasy of Israel
   Hosea 2:13; 4:12, 17; Amos 5:21-26

   _____

   _____

   _____

d. The social inequality in Israel
   Amos 2:6; 5:11

   _____

e. The moral depravity of Israel
   Hosea 4:1, 2

   _____

   _____

LESSON 22   OBADIAH—JONAH—MICAH

In the blank space at the right-hand margin write "True" or "False" after each of the following statements:

13. Jonah did not want to go to Nineveh for the fulfillment of the will of God for his life. _____

14. The Gentile city against which Jonah prophesied repented permanently. _____

15. Micah prophesied to both Israel and Judah. _____

16. Micah's prophecies embrace the then distant future as well as his own times. _____

17. Obadiah expressed personal hatred and bigotry in denouncing Edom. _____

18. Name the kings, prophets or event indicated on this chart by the following letters:

    a. _____

    b. _____

    c. _____

    d. _____

    e. _____

    f. _____

Judah	Prophets	Israel	World Powers
Jehoram 848-841 B.C.	? A ?	Jehoram	• F
Ahaziah			
Athaliah		Jehu	
Joash		Jehoahaz	
		Jehoash	
Amaziah	? C ?	E	
Uzziah		Zachariah	
		Shallum	
		Menahem	
	?	Pekahiah	• 2½ tribes east of Jordan taken captive by Assyria
D		Pekah	
Ahaz	B ISAIAH	Hoshea	• Fall of Samaria 722 B.C. Assyrian captivity begins
Hezekiah		Assyrian captivity	• Assyrians invade Judah God intervenes to save Jerusalem

281

19. Name the places on this map which are connected with the story of Jonah.

   a. _____

   b. _____

   c. _____

   MAP SHOWING THE FLIGHT OF JONAH "FROM THE PRESENCE OF THE LORD"

Dig Deeper in Your Bible

You may use your Bible to complete the remainder of this exam.

20. Look up the following Scriptures. Then cross out the false statements in the brackets. When you have finished, you will have a brief history of the Edomites.

   EXAMPLE:

   [Obadiah; ~~Hosea~~] *prophesied against the Edomites.*

   a. The Edomites were descended from [Esau; Amalek] (Genesis 36:6-9).

   b. Their land was sometimes called [Mount Sinai; Mount Seir] (Genesis 36:8).

   c. It was given to them by God (Joshua 24:2-4). Yet, like the Israelites, they had to drive out the original inhabitants. These were known as [the Horims; the Hivites] (Deuteronomy 2:12).

   d. When the Israelites asked permission to cross their country en route to Canaan, the Edomites [agreed; refused] (Numbers 20:18-21).

e. They were attacked and defeated by Saul some 400 years later (I Samuel 14:47) and then again by David. On this occasion Joab [spared; exterminated] most of the male population of the country (I Kings 11:15, 16) and placed Jewish garrisons in all their strongholds (II Samuel 8:13, 14).

f. Hadad, the Edomite, escaped at this time and afterward became [a bosom friend; a bitter foe] of Solomon (I Kings 11:14-25).

g. In the days of Jehoram, king of Judah, the Edomites gained their independence (II Chronicles 21:8-10) and in the days of King [Ahaz; Hezekiah] the Edomites began to give vent to their hatred of the Jews (II Chronicles 28:16, 17).

h. When Nebuchadnezzar invaded Judea, the Edomites joined him and took an active part in the plunder of Jerusalem and the slaughter of the Jews. Their cruelty at that time is referred to in [Psalm 137; Psalm 147].

Nebuchadnezzar allowed the Edomites to settle in southern Palestine. Later they were driven out of Edom proper by the Nabataeans. When the Jewish state was reborn, they were again subdued by the Jews and forced to conform to Jewish laws and rites. They were known by Greek and Roman writers as the Idumaeans. Herod the Great was an Idumaean. When the Romans sacked Jerusalem in A.D. 70, many Idumaeans avenged themselves upon the Jews; but from that time, they vanished from the page of history as a separate people.

Reading Chart

Check (×) the chapters you have read.

	HOSEA					5				10
	JOEL									
	AMOS					5				
	OBADIAH									
	JONAH									
	MICAH					5				

_____MAIL TO ADDRESS ON BACK COVER.

284

Lesson 23

Nahum—Habakkuk—Zephaniah

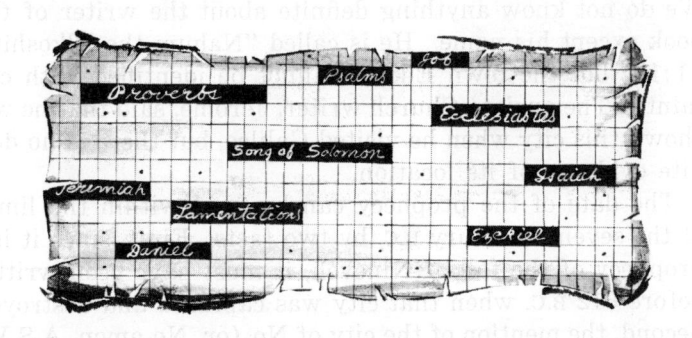

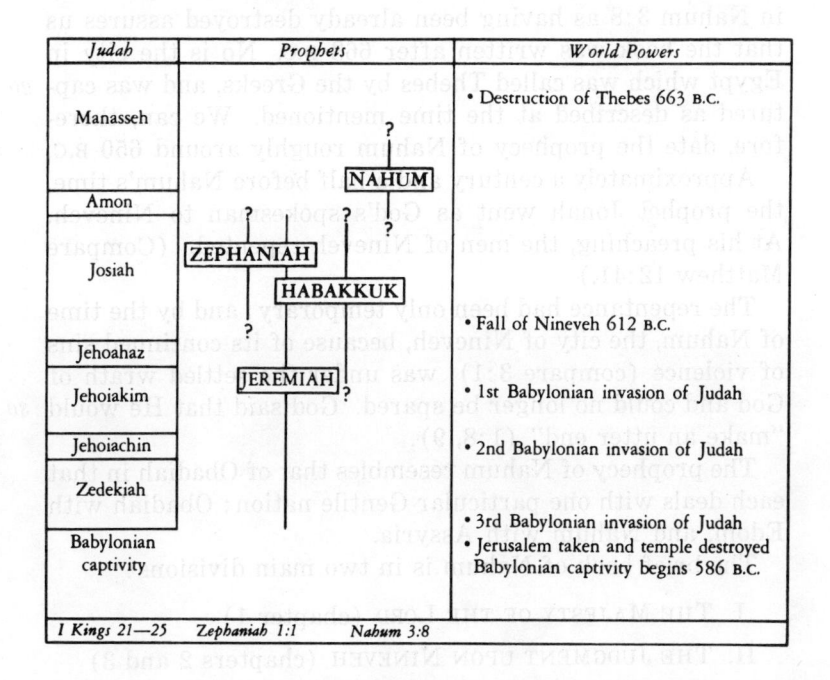

Judah	Prophets	World Powers
Manasseh		• Destruction of Thebes 663 B.C.
Amon	? NAHUM ?	
Josiah	ZEPHANIAH ? HABAKKUK	
Jehoahaz	?	• Fall of Nineveh 612 B.C.
Jehoiakim	JEREMIAH ?	• 1st Babylonian invasion of Judah
Jehoiachin		• 2nd Babylonian invasion of Judah
Zedekiah		
Babylonian captivity		• 3rd Babylonian invasion of Judah • Jerusalem taken and temple destroyed Babylonian captivity begins 586 B.C.
I Kings 21—25	Zephaniah 1:1	Nahum 3:8

285

The brief books which we are to study in this lesson are all prophecies of the latter half of the seventh century B.C. By that time the Kingdom of Israel had long since been destroyed, and the Kingdom of Judah was nearing its doom at the hand of the Babylonians.

NAHUM

We do not know anything definite about the writer of this book except his name. He is called "Nahum the Elkoshite" (1:1); but the town Elkosh cannot be identified with certainty. The ancient Church writer, Jerome, said that he was shown this city when he visited Galilee, but there is no definite evidence of its location.

The date of the prophecy can be fixed within the limits of the seventh century B.C. by two facts. First, since it is a prophecy of the fall of Nineveh, it must have been written before 612 B.C. when that city was captured and destroyed. Second, the mention of the city of No (or, No-amon, A.S.V.) in Nahum 3:8 as having been already destroyed assures us that the book was written after 663 B.C. No is the city in Egypt which was called Thebes by the Greeks, and was captured as described at the time mentioned. We can, therefore, date the prophecy of Nahum roughly around 650 B.C.

Approximately a century and a half before Nahum's time, the prophet Jonah went as God's spokesman to Nineveh. At his preaching, the men of Nineveh repented. (Compare Matthew 12:41.)

The repentance had been only temporary; and by the time of Nahum, the city of Nineveh, because of its continued sins of violence (compare 3:1), was under the settled wrath of God and could no longer be spared. God said that He would "make an utter end" (1:8, 9).

The prophecy of Nahum resembles that of Obadiah in that each deals with one particular Gentile nation: Obadiah with Edom, and Nahum with Assyria.

The brief book of Nahum is in two main divisions:

    I. THE MAJESTY OF THE LORD (chapter 1)

    II. THE JUDGMENT UPON NINEVEH (chapters 2 and 3)

The first division is a great poetic section describing the character and power of the Lord. God is seen as slow to anger but as One who will not acquit the wicked (1:3). One who trusts in Him is encouraged by this marvelous description: "The LORD is good, a stronghold in the day of trouble; and he knoweth them that trust in him" (1:7). At the close of the chapter Judah is pictured as receiving the message concerning the destruction of its dreadful enemy, Assyria.

The second division of the book describes, among other things, the battle for Nineveh. The city was brought to its doom by a coalition of the Medes and the Babylonians, assisted by the swollen Tigris River (as prophesied in 2:6). The terrible sins of Nineveh brought inevitable punishment from God. The ruins of this once-mighty city furnished new testimony to the truthfulness of God's Word.

HABAKKUK

The prophecy of Habakkuk was probably given late in the reign of King Josiah or early in the reign of Jehoiakim, possibly around 610 B.C. Nothing is known of the prophet himself; but one well-known expression from his prophecy (2:4) furnishes an important text for three great New Testament epistles (Romans 1:17; Galatians 3:11; Hebrews 10:38).

The prophet questions God and, in fact, complains about what he considers to be injustice. God answers him and foretells the coming capture of the Kingdom of Judah by the Babylonians. The book is in two main parts:

I. THE PROPHET'S COMPLAINT AND GOD'S ANSWER (chapters 1 and 2)

II. THE PROPHET'S PRAYER (chapter 3)

Habakkuk's cry is one of bewilderment that God is seemingly indifferent to the iniquities abounding in Judah. God answers that He will work a work of judgment in bringing the Chaldeans, "that bitter and hasty nation," as His instrument of chastisement upon the wicked people of Judah. This causes Habakkuk even greater perplexity, for he cannot understand the righteousness of punishing a sinful nation by means of a nation even more sinful. How can God do this, in view of the fact that He is "of purer eyes than to behold evil" and cannot "look on iniquity" (1:13)? The prophet then awaits God's reply, which begins in 2:2. The LORD promises future relief and deliverance for His people and urges them to have patience, and wait, for it will surely come (2:3). And He further assures the prophet that the sinful Babylonian nation, although an instrument of His judgment upon Judah, will not escape His righteous judgment for its own sins. God is the sovereign Lord of history, and no nation can escape accountability to Him. "But the LORD is in his holy temple: let all the earth keep silence before him" (2:20).

The prophet's prayer (chapter 3) recalls God's past works in the early history of the nation of Israel, and expresses Habakkuk's own faith and confidence in God. That this confidence is not in God's blessing or the things which God gives but in the Lord Himself, is shown by the prophet's description of complete adversity and his triumphant assertion, "Yet I will rejoice in the LORD, I will joy in the God of my salvation" (3:18). An echo of this is heard in the words of Paul to the Philippians, "Rejoice in the Lord alway: and again I say, Rejoice" (Philippians 4:4). The prophet finds the complete answer to his perplexity in God Himself, just as Job found God to be the solution of his problem.

ZEPHANIAH

The writer of this prophecy is the only one of the prophets who gives his ancestry for several generations. It is likely that the reason for this is that the Hizkiah of 1:1 was actually King Hezekiah, and that the prophet Zephaniah is thus showing his own connection with the royal family of Judah. (The A.S.V. spelling in Zephaniah 1:1 is *Hezekiah*.) If this view is correct, he was a distant cousin, or relative, of the king of his own day, Josiah. This prophecy must have been given about 630 B.C., since it was declared to be in the days of Josiah. This would make Zephaniah a contemporary of the prophet Jeremiah, who began his ministry in the thirteenth year of the reign of King Josiah.

The prophecy of Zephaniah is similar to that of Joel in the sense that both of these writers have as their theme "the day of the LORD." God, through the prophet, describes that coming day as a "day of wrath" (1:15), and speaks of His "fierce anger" (2:2; 3:8). This fierce anger of the LORD is further described as "the fire of his jealousy" (1:18), and the "fire of my jealousy" (3:8).

Undoubtedly there is a foreshadowing of this coming "day of the LORD" in Nebuchadnezzar's invasion of Judah within the prophet's own lifetime. We have seen in other writings of the prophets that often the near view and the far view are mingled together.

The book has three main sections:

I. JUDGMENT UPON JUDAH (chapters 1—2:3)
II. JUDGMENT UPON THE NATIONS (chapters 2:4—3:8)
III. ULTIMATE DELIVERANCE FOR JUDAH (chapter 3:9-20)

In the first section of the prophecy, God pronounces His judgment upon Judah (chapter 1). The immediate judgment is to come through the Babylonian invasion; but, as has been said before, this trouble looks forward to the greater judgment of the end time. This section closes with an appeal to those who are described as the "meek of the earth," that they may seek the LORD and thus be hid in the day of His anger (2:3).

The second section concerns judgment upon the nations (2:4—3:8). As in some of the other prophets, various surrounding nations are described as subject to the judgment of God, but Judah will not escape. We see her described at the beginning of chapter 3.

But there will be ultimate deliverance for Judah, as the closing section demonstrates (3:9-20). Even as "the just LORD," when He was in the midst of the sinful city, could bring only punishment, so the same LORD "in the midst" of the cleansed and restored city (3:17) will bring great joy and blessing.

While these Old Testament prophecies may seem to have little relationship to our lives, yet we can see in all of them the principle of God's righteousness, which must punish sin; and we can see God's grace, which provides salvation for those who trust Him.

Self Check Test 12

What do you remember about Nahum, Habakkuk and Zephaniah?

In the right-hand column circle the following statements "true" or "false":

1. Zephaniah foretold the ultimate blessing and restoration of Assyria. (p. 289)   T   F

2. The books of Nahum, Habakkuk, and Zephaniah all relate to the latter half of the seventeenth century B.C. (p. 286)   T   F

3. Nineveh was to be judged because of its sins of violence. (p. 286)   T   F

4. The prophet Habakkuk finds a complete answer to his problem in the story of Job. (p. 288)   T   F

5. Zephaniah was a contemporary of the prophet Isaiah. (p. 289)   T   F

6. Jeremiah and Nahum both prophesied to Nineveh. (p. 286)   T   F

7. The Greeks and Romans formed the coalition which overthrew Nineveh. (p. 287)   T   F

8. Habakkuk was puzzled by the prophecies of Malachi. (pp. 287, 288)   T   F

9. Habakkuk and Zephaniah lived and prophesied in the days of King Josiah. (pp. 287-289)   T   F

10. There were three Babylonian invasions of Judah. (chart, p. 285)   T   F

11. Give the dates of the following events:

   a. The destruction of Nineveh (p. 286) _____

   b. The destruction of Thebes (p. 286) _____

   c. The approximate time Nahum was written (p. 286) _____

   d. The probable time Habakkuk was written (p. 287) _____

   e. The approximate time Zephaniah was written (p. 288) _____

12. *Complete the following outlines:*

   NAHUM   *Chapters*

   I. _____   1

   II. _____   2 and 3
   (p. 286)

   HABAKKUK

   I. _____   1 and 2

   II. _____   3
   (p. 287)

   ZEPHANIAH

   I. Judgment upon Judah   _____

   II. Judgment upon the Nations   _____

   III. Ultimate Deliverance for Judah (p. 289)   _____

Turn to page 310 to find the correct answers.
Please do not send the answers to the Correspondence School.

Lesson 24

Haggai—Zechariah—Malachi

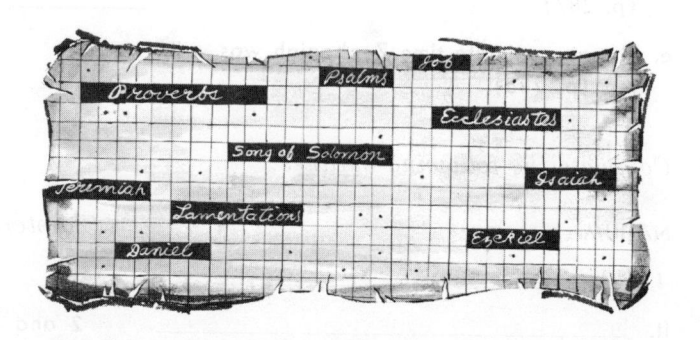

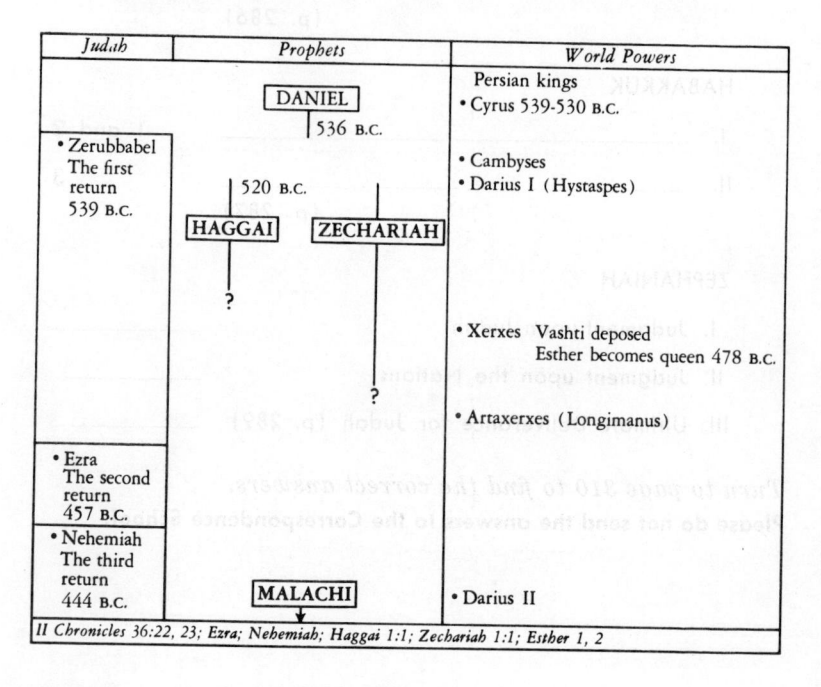

Judah	Prophets	World Powers
	DANIEL — 536 B.C.	Persian kings • Cyrus 539-530 B.C.
• Zerubbabel The first return 539 B.C.	520 B.C. HAGGAI ZECHARIAH ? ?	• Cambyses • Darius I (Hystaspes)
		• Xerxes Vashti deposed Esther becomes queen 478 B.C.
		• Artaxerxes (Longimanus)
• Ezra The second return 457 B.C. • Nehemiah The third return 444 B.C.	MALACHI	• Darius II
II Chronicles 36:22, 23; Ezra; Nehemiah; Haggai 1:1; Zechariah 1:1; Esther 1, 2		

292

The prophets considered in this lesson are the only three known as postexilic. That is, they lived and ministered after the Babylonian captivity. Both Haggai and Zechariah were contemporary with Zerubbabel at the time of the return from Babylon. Malachi belonged to a later generation and was probably contemporary with Ezra and Nehemiah.

HAGGAI

When Cyrus issued the decree permitting the Jews to return from captivity to Jerusalem (539 B.C.), a number went back under the leadership of Zerubbabel and Joshua, the high priest. (See Ezra 1:1—2:70.) Shortly after arriving in Jerusalem, they laid the foundation for a new temple; but because of the opposition of other people living in the land, the work on the temple was discontinued for many years. Haggai was a messenger of God to encourage the people to resume the work on the temple and to finish it. We read of him in Ezra 5:1.

Haggai gives the precise dates of his prophecies, all of which were in the latter part of the second year of Darius, the Persian king, that is, in 520 B.C. His book is a practical message for the people of his own time, exhorting them to complete the work of the Temple, although the prophecy does look forward to future blessings under the Messiah. Haggai 2:7 is undoubtedly a reference to the Lord Jesus Christ, called here "the desire of all nations."

God, through the prophet, asks searching questions of His people, calling attention to the fact that they have neglected Him in failing to resume the building of the temple. His exhortation is, "Consider your ways" (1:5, 7).

The brief prophecy is in *four different addresses*. *The first* of these rebukes the people for their negligence and calls upon them to build the house (1:8). God tells them that much of their distress and lack of prosperity is a result of their neglect of the LORD and of His house. This initial message of the prophet brought a ready response from Zerubbabel and the people.

The second message (2:1-9) considers the fact that the

293

temple now being built did not seem to compare in magnificence with the former temple of Solomon; but it is also a call to be strong and courageous in view of God's promise that ultimately the glory of this house will be greater than that of the other (2:9) because of the presence of the Son of God during His earthly ministry.

The third message of Haggai (2:10-19) is addressed to the priests (2:11), and calls upon them to separate themselves unto the LORD. *The fourth message* is a word for Zerubbabel (2:20-23). This godly governor is seen as a type or prophetic symbol of the Lord Jesus Christ, through whom God will "overthrow the throne of kingdoms" (2:22). Thus God blends the present and the future by exhortation and promise.

ZECHARIAH

Zechariah is mentioned along with Haggai in Ezra 5:1 and 6:14. He began his ministry in the same year that Haggai prophesied. (Compare Zechariah 1:1 with Haggai 1:1.) Like Haggai, Zechariah had a practical message to the people of his time concerning the building of the temple and obedience to God, but his prophecy is much more extensive than that of Haggai. It forms, in fact, a résumé of Messianic prophecy, gathering together and repeating predictions concerning Christ found in some of the prophets of an earlier time. His prophecy is broad in its scope, including both the first and second advents of Christ, and describing the millennial kingdom.

The key phrase of this book is the expression, "the LORD of hosts" (used fifty-two times), a description of God as the Leader and Ruler of the heavenly armies.

The book of Zechariah is in three main divisions.

   I. EIGHT VISIONS, FOLLOWED BY THE SYMBOLIC CROWNING OF JOSHUA (chapters 1—6)

   II. QUESTION CONCERNING FASTING, WITH INSTRUCTION FROM GOD (chapters 7 and 8)

   III. END TIME PROPHECIES DELIVERED AS TWO "BURDENS" (chapters 9—14)

1. The Eight Visions (chapters 1—6)

Zechariah, as a young man (2:4), is called upon to remind his generation of the messages of "the former prophets" (1:4). God gives him eight visions, apparently all in the same night.

In the *first* of these visions, *the man among the myrtle trees* (1:8-11), is seen God's judgment of the nations because of their oppression of Israel. God is "very sore displeased with the heathen" (1:15).

This judgment upon the nations is further depicted in the *second* vision (1:18-21), that of *the four horns and the four carpenters* (A.S.V., four smiths). The horns are the nations which have scattered Judah and Israel, and the smiths represent God's judgment upon them.

The *third* vision of *the man with the measuring line* (2:1-13) promises future enlargement and blessing for Jerusalem, with God in the midst of her.

The *fourth* vision of *the cleansing of Joshua, the high priest,* is prophetic of Israel's future cleansing (3:1-10). There is also here, by application, a picture of the cleansing of the individual sinner through God's gracious salvation. The sinner's condition is seen (3:3). Satan is opposing him (3:1), but God had chosen him (3:2). God's salvation leads to a glorious transformation in his life (3:4, 5), and that is followed by service for God (3:6, 7). The deliverance of the individual sinner and the future deliverance of God's people Israel are accomplished through the One who is called in the passage, God's "servant the Branch" (3:8, A.S.V.).

The picture of *the candlestick (lampstand) and two olive trees,* comprising the *fifth* vision (4:1-14), describes witnessing in the power of the Spirit of God. The olive trees furnish a continual supply of oil for the lampstand in God's temple. This is a symbolic picture of the work of the Spirit of God: "Not by might, nor by power, but by my spirit saith the LORD of hosts" (4:6). The "two anointed ones" (4:14) evidently were, in the prophet's day, Zerubbabel, the governor; and Joshua, the high priest. In the book of Revelation God speaks of two witnesses like these who will testify for Him in the end time (Revelation 11:3, 4).

The last three visions all have to do with *God's judgment*. In the vision of *the flying roll* (5:1-4) God's law is seen as bringing judgment upon His people. The vision of *the woman in the ephah*[1] (5:5-11) shows that God must judge the elements of Babylonianism still remaining in His people. In Babylon the people of Israel had learned a greedy commercialism which has plagued them ever since, and which God will judge. The closing vision of *the four chariots* shows God's judgment upon the nation through various destructive agencies under His control (6:1-8).

This section of the book closes with the symbolic crowning of Joshua, the high priest. He is seen as a type of "the man whose name is the Branch" (6:12, A.S.V.), that is, the Lord Jesus Christ, who will combine in His Person the offices of King and Priest.

2. Question Concerning Fasting (chapters 7 and 8)

In the second division of the book, the question is raised by the people concerning fasting. God shows them that much of their fasting for certain occasions was mere formalism, and was not for Him. Far more important than such ceremonial fasting, is this: hearing and doing the Word of God. If His people obey Him, their fast will be turned into a feast. God will bless them, and His blessings will flow out from them to other nations as well.

3. End Time Prophecies (chapters 9—14)

In the closing division of the book, God speaks of judgment, both upon other nations and upon His own people Israel. In this section are a number of well-known prophecies of the Lord Jesus Christ, notably the one concerning His entry into Jerusalem when He presented

---

[1]The ephah was a Hebrew measure equal to about six or seven gallons, and probably the ancient Jewish symbol for trade.

Himself as King (9:9; compare Matthew 21:1-10; Mark 11:1-10; Luke 19:28-40; John 12:12-15). Here, as in many other prophecies, the two advents of Christ are blended. Some of the promises concern events that can take place only in connection with the return of the Lord. Jerusalem's extremity in the end time, under the persecution of Antichrist, is described (see chapter 12), followed by the national cleansing of Israel (13:1). The coming of Christ in glory and the setting up of His Kingdom over all the earth are foretold in chapter 14. In many respects Zechariah echoes his great predecessor, Isaiah. Both say much of Christ and magnify Him.

MALACHI

Malachi, the latest of the writing prophets, is personally unknown. His name means "my messenger." He lived and ministered several generations after Haggai and Zechariah, probably in the time of Nehemiah, close to the year 400 B.C.

Malachi eloquently reminds us that the battle with sin is never ended in this life. Although the people of Israel had been cured of idolatry in the Babylonian captivity, they still were unfaithful to God. Much of their worship was mere form, filled with insincerity and hypocrisy. After beginning with a statement of God's love for Israel (1:1-5), the prophet describes the sins of the priests (1:6—2:9) and the sins of the people generally (2:10—3:15). They are so lacking in moral sense that they seem to be unaware of the nature of many of their sins, for they repeatedly ask God why He judges them.

In the midst of the section on the sins of the people God interjects a promise concerning two messengers (3:1): one, the forerunner of the Messiah, identified in the New Testament as John the Baptizer (compare Matthew 11:10; Mark 1:2; Luke 7:27); and the other, the Lord Jesus Christ Himself, the "messenger of the covenant."

In contrast to the people generally, is the God-fearing remnant described in 3:16—4:6. Christ is seen as the "Sun of righteousness" (4:2), and this book, as well as the whole Old Testament, closes with a note of expectation. The Old

Testament is perfect in every part, since it is from God; but it is incomplete, awaiting fulfillment in the events of the New Testament.

REVIEW EXERCISE

NOTE: You will not be able to complete Exam 12 unless you fill in the blank spaces on the REVIEW CHART, page 299. Using as your guide the charts which appear with each lesson on the prophets, fill in on the REVIEW CHART the missing names of the kings, prophets, and Hebrew leaders.

Upon the completion of this chart, you will have before you a good overview of the Old Testament prophets as they are related to their historical background.

REVIEW CHART

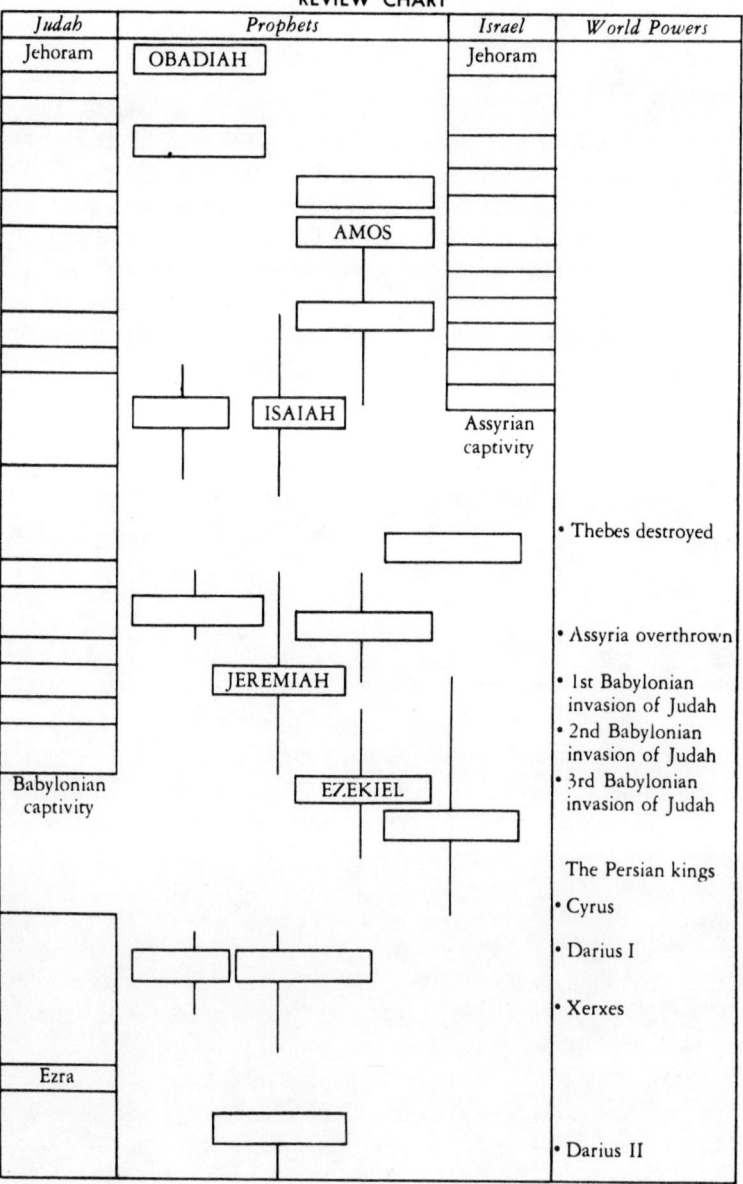

Judah	Prophets	Israel	World Powers
Jehoram	OBADIAH	Jehoram	
	AMOS		
		Assyrian captivity	
	ISAIAH		
			• Thebes destroyed
			• Assyria overthrown
	JEREMIAH		• 1st Babylonian invasion of Judah
			• 2nd Babylonian invasion of Judah
Babylonian captivity	EZEKIEL		• 3rd Babylonian invasion of Judah
			The Persian kings
			• Cyrus
			• Darius I
			• Xerxes
Ezra			
			• Darius II

Survey of the Scriptures
A Moody Correspondence Course

Exam 12
Lessons 23, 24

Name_____ (Print plainly) Exam Grade_____

Address_____ Date_____

City_____ State_____ Zip Code_____ Class Number_____

Instructor_____

LESSON 23 NAHUM—HABAKKUK—ZEPHANIAH

In the blank space at the right-hand margin write "True" or "False" after each of the following statements:

1. Both Zephaniah and Joel have as their theme "the day of the LORD." _____

2. The invasion of Judah by Nebuchadnezzar fulfilled Zephaniah's prophecy in full. _____

3. Zephaniah prophesied exclusively concerning Judah. _____

4. Habakkuk was perplexed that a righteous God could chastise sinful Judah by means of an even more sinful nation. _____

In the blank space write the letter of the correct or most nearly correct answer.

5. The prophet who had a similar ministry to that of Nahum was

    a. Jeremiah.
    b. Jonah.
    c. Joel.
    d. Jude. _____

6. The coalition which brought about the downfall of Nineveh was that of the

    a. Medes and Babylonians.
    b. Medes and Persians.
    c. Babylonians and Assyrians.
    d. Greeks and Romans. _____

7. The prophet Habakkuk was puzzled by

    a. an apparent injustice in God's dealings.
    b. the cruelty of the Assyrians.
    c. the overthrow of Memphis.
    d. the prophecies of Jeremiah. _____

8. The well-known expression of Habakkuk which is repeated three times in the New Testament has to do with

    a. faith.
    b. hope.
    c. love.
    d. mercy. _____

9. Zephaniah is thought to have been a descendant of King

    a. Zachariah.
    b. Pekahiah.
    c. Hoshea.
    d. Hezekiah. _____

10. Name the prophets and events indicated on this chart by the following letters:

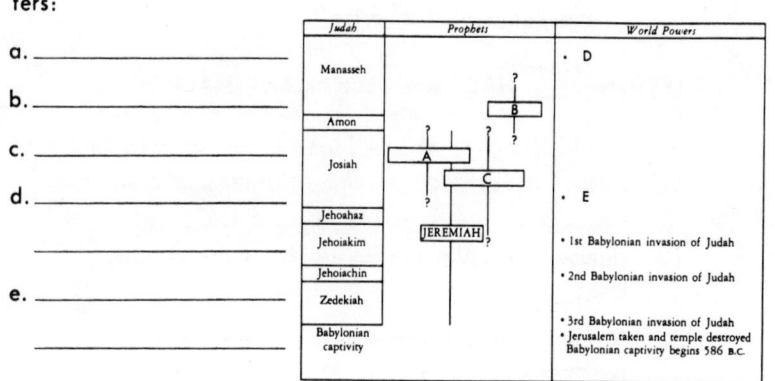

a. _____

b. _____

c. _____

d. _____
_____

e. _____
_____

Judah	Prophets	World Powers
Manasseh	? B	• D
Amon	? ? ?	
Josiah	A C	
Jehoahaz	?	• E
Jehoiakim	JEREMIAH ?	• 1st Babylonian invasion of Judah
Jehoiachin		• 2nd Babylonian invasion of Judah
Zedekiah		
Babylonian captivity		• 3rd Babylonian invasion of Judah • Jerusalem taken and temple destroyed Babylonian captivity begins 586 B.C.

Use Your Bible

You may use your Bible to answer the next question.

11. Both Habakkuk and Zephaniah lived and prophesied in the days of King Josiah. Read II Kings 21:19—24:4 and answer the following questions, which are designed to give you the historical background for their prophecies.

   a. Did Josiah have a godly father? _____

   b. Who was the high priest in the days of Josiah? _____

   c. What great work did Josiah have undertaken in the eighteenth year of his reign? _____

   d. What important discovery did the high priest make? _____

   e. Was the nation very deeply apostate at the time of Josiah's reformation? _____

   f. Who was the prophetess who dwelt in the Jerusalem college? _____

   g. In whose reign was Josiah named before his birth? (See I Kings 13:1-3.) _____

   h. Was Josiah one of the greatest of all the reforming kings of Judah? _____

i. Was the religious revival which began under Josiah permanent? _____

j. Did it save Judah from the growing threat of the Babylonian invasion? _____

LESSON 24   HAGGAI—ZECHARIAH—MALACHI

In the blank space at the right-hand margin write "True" or "False" after each of the following statements:

12. Haggai gives the precise dates of his prophecies. _____

13. Haggai was concerned because the returned remnant were neglecting to build the Temple. _____

14. Zechariah repeats predictions concerning Christ found in earlier prophecies. _____

15. Malachi probably ministered about 400 B.C. _____

16. "The messenger of the covenant" is the apostle Paul. _____

17. Zechariah foretold Christ's triumphal entry into Jerusalem. _____

In the blank space write the letter of the correct or most nearly correct answer.

18. Malachi tells us that
    a. the name of Christ's forerunner is John the Baptizer.
    b. the battle with sin is never ended in this life.
    c. much of the fasting in Israel was mere formalism.
    d. the Temple in Jerusalem was equally as glorious as that originally built by Solomon. _____

19. The postexilic prophets who ministered at the same time were

    a. Malachi and Zechariah.
    b. Haggai and Zechariah.
    c. Haggai and Malachi.
    d. None of them.   _____

20. The Jews who returned from captivity when Cyrus gave his decree did so under the leadership of

    a. Zerubbabel and Ezra.
    b. Joshua and Caleb.
    c. Ezra and Nehemiah.
    d. Zerubbabel and Joshua.   _____

21. The phrase which occurs 52 times in Zechariah is

    a. the God of Jacob.
    b. the LORD of hosts.
    c. the King of kings.
    d. My Servant the Branch.   _____

22. The last three of Zechariah's visions have to do with

    a. blessing.
    b. peace.
    c. prosperity.
    d. judgment.   _____

23. Name the leaders, prophets and event indicated on this chart by the following letters:

a. _____

b. _____
   _____

c. _____
   _____

d. _____

e. _____

f. _____

Judah	Prophets	World Powers
	DANIEL 536 B.C.	Persian kings • D
A	520 B.C. E F ?	• Cambyses • Darius I (Hystaspes)
	?	• Xerxes Vashti deposed Esther becomes queen 478 B.C. • Artaxerxes (Longimanus)
B		
C	MALACHI	• Darius II

24. On page 299 of your textbook you will find a REVIEW CHART which you should have completed in connection with the REVIEW EXERCISE on page 298. Compare the chart you completed with the one which occurs on page 307 of this exam. In the blank spaces below list four mistakes which appear on the chart in the exam.

EXAMPLE: *The kings Ahaziah to Amon of Judah are listed as kings of Israel and kings Jehu to Hoshea of Israel are listed as kings of Judah.*

a. _____

b. _____

c. _____

d. _____

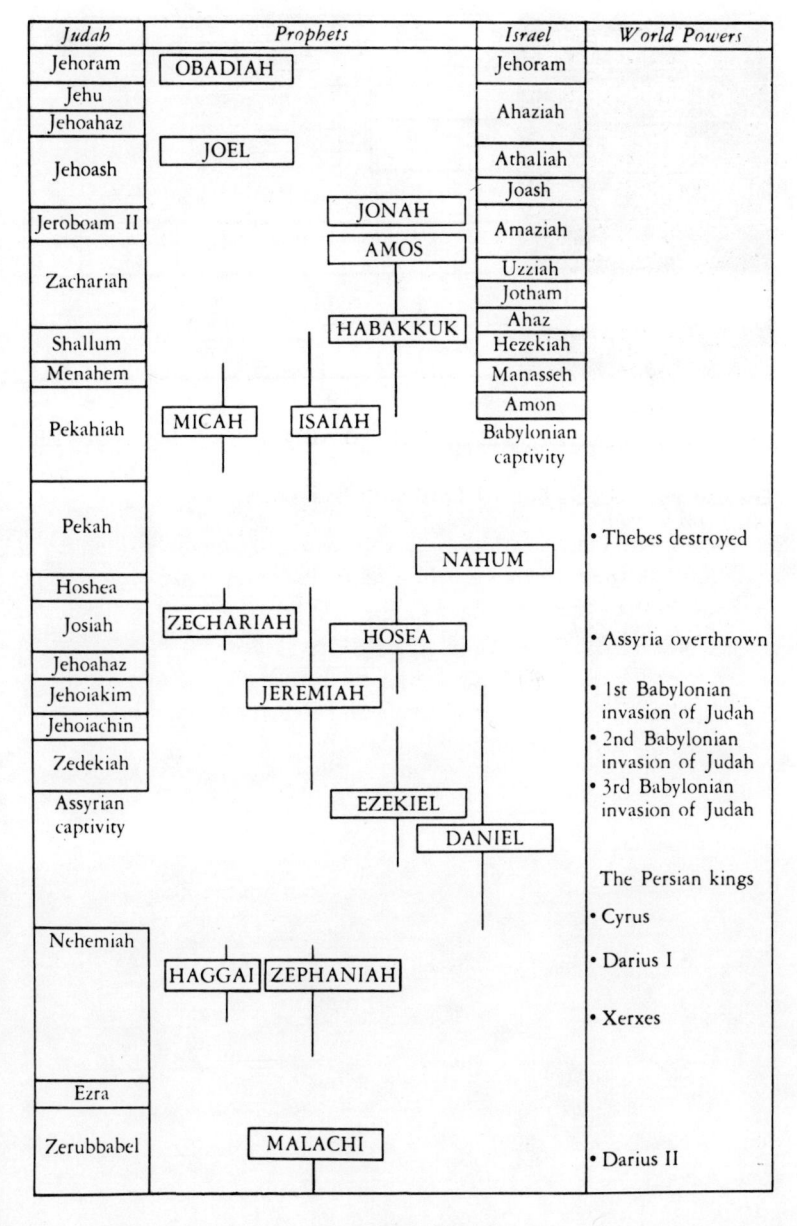

Judah	Prophets	Israel	World Powers
Jehoram	OBADIAH	Jehoram	
Jehu		Ahaziah	
Jehoahaz			
Jehoash	JOEL	Athaliah	
		Joash	
Jeroboam II	JONAH	Amaziah	
	AMOS		
Zachariah		Uzziah	
		Jotham	
	HABAKKUK	Ahaz	
Shallum		Hezekiah	
Menahem		Manasseh	
Pekahiah	MICAH ISAIAH	Amon	
		Babylonian captivity	
Pekah			• Thebes destroyed
Hoshea	NAHUM		
Josiah	ZECHARIAH HOSEA		• Assyria overthrown
Jehoahaz			
Jehoiakim	JEREMIAH		• 1st Babylonian invasion of Judah
Jehoiachin			• 2nd Babylonian invasion of Judah
Zedekiah			• 3rd Babylonian invasion of Judah
Assyrian captivity	EZEKIEL		
	DANIEL		
			The Persian kings
			• Cyrus
Nehemiah	HAGGAI ZEPHANIAH		• Darius I
			• Xerxes
Ezra			
Zerubbabel	MALACHI		• Darius II

Reading Chart

Check (×) the chapters you have read.

NAHUM									
HABAKKUK									
ZEPHANIAH									
HAGGAI									
ZECHARIAH					5				10
MALACHI									

_____MAIL TO ADDRESS ON BACK COVER.

Enclose your Grade Record Card with this exam.

Answer Key to Self-check Tests

CHECK-UP TIME

Test 7   True: **1**   False: **2, 3, 4, 5**
Lesson 13   **6** c, **7** a, **8** b, **9** a, **10** a, **11** b, **12** a

Test 8   True: **1, 2, 6, 7, 8, 9**   False: **3, 4, 5, 10**
Lesson 15   **11** c, **12** a
            13 1:9 or 1:14; 2:3, 11, 17, 18, 19, 20 or 2:22; 3:16;
            4:1, 3, 7, 15; 5:13, 18; 6:1, 12; 8:9, 15 (twice), 17;
            9:3, 6, 9, 9, 11, 13; 10:5

Test 9   True: **3, 4, 5, 6, 7**   False: **1, 2**
Lesson 17   **8** 49-57; **9** 53; **10** 6, 7; **11** 7
            12-16 Egypt, Moab, Arabia, Tyre

Test 10   True: **2, 3, 7, 10**   False: **1, 4, 5, 6, 8, 9**
Lesson 19   **11** c, **12** a, **13** c

Test 11   True: **2, 3, 5**   False: **1, 4, 6, 7, 8, 9, 10**
Lesson 21   **11** Hosea   I. The Prophet's Experience
                            II. The Prophet's Teaching

            Joel   I. The Plague of Insects and "the Day of
                        the LORD"
                     II. Blessing and Judgment in the Last Days

            Amos   I. Judgment on the Nations
                     II. Punishment of Israel for Iniquity
                     III. Visions of Judgment
            12 c, e, b, a, d

309

Test 12   True: **3, 9, 10**   False: **1, 2, 4, 5, 6, 7, 8**
Lesson 23 **11** a, 612 B.C.; b, 663 B.C.; c, 650 B.C.; d, 610 B.C.;
           e, 630 B.C.
           12 Nahum   I. The Majesty of the LORD
                           II. The Judgment upon Nineveh

                Habakkuk   I. The Prophet's Complaint and God's Answer
                           II. The Prophet's Prayer

                Zephaniah   I. 1
                           II. 2:4—3:8
                          III. 3:9-20

How well did you do?

Fewer than four wrong answers—excellent work
Four or more wrong answers—restudy the lesson